REALITIES OF AZERBAIJAN
1917-1920

Realities Of Azerbaijan
1917-1920

ANAR ISGENDERLI

Library of Congress Control Number:		2011903484
ISBN:	Hardcover	978-1-4568-7954-9
	Softcover	978-1-4568-7953-2
	Ebook	978-1-4568-7955-6

First published in 2011.

Isgenderli, Anar—
Realities of Azerbaijan: 1917-1920

Foreword by Justin McCarthy

Translated by Yusif Axundov

© Anar Isgenderli, 2011

This book was printed in the United States of America.

To order additional copies of this book, contact:
Xlibris Corporation
1-888-795-4274
www.Xlibris.com
Orders@Xlibris.com
75308

CONTENTS

It should not be possible any longer to write the history of atrocity and inhumanity without including the losses of the Turks of Azerbaijan.

—Prof. Justin McCarthy

FOREWORD

THE HISTORY OF the suffering of the Turks of the Southern Caucasus has been little known. Some historians have written of the military aspects of Russian campaigns, but not of the effect of the Russian conquest on the people of the region: Baddeley's monumental *The Russian Conquest of the Caucasus* is a catalog of battles and politics. Allen and Muratoff's *Caucasian Battlefields* devotes only the occasional sentence to massacre and forced migration, stressing the suffering of Armenians. With few exceptions, Armenian historians make very limited reference to Turkish refugees and even more limited mention of Turkish deaths. Standard textbooks do not consider the deaths and forced migration of Azerbaijani Turks at all and often avoid mention of even the existence of Azerbaijan.

Realities of Azerbaijan is a corrective to the long neglect of a history of great significance. The book's strength lies in its Russian, Turkish, and Azerbaijani sources, often sources that have been seen in no other studies. They relate a history much at odds with the conventional belief that only Armenians suffered. For the historical record, the most important section of the book is chapter 3. It relates, in great detail, the slaughter of Turks in Azerbaijan and Armenia. It is not a cheerful reading. Relation of slaughter following upon slaughter can never be enjoyable. Yet the long list of inhumanities is the stuff of accurate history. It tells us that the death and exile of the people of Azerbaijan is one of the great human disasters.

Realities of Azerbaijan will hopefully not be the last study of the slaughters of Azerbaijan. Those writing on the period of World War I and on the Turkish-Armenian conflict have a new source for balanced histories. It should not be possible any longer to write the history of atrocity and inhumanity without including the losses of the Turks of Azerbaijan.

Justin McCarthy
Professor of History and Distinguished University Scholar,
University of Louisville

INTRODUCTION

THE ANCIENT INDIGENOUS peoples of the region, now known as the Azerbaijanis, had generally benevolent relations with their neighbors. It is known that in the middle of the third millennium BC, the Azerbaijani tribes of Guti, Turukku, and Lullubi established close trade relations with their neighbors, including tribes of Mesopotamia. The ninth century BC was marked by the formation of an ancient state of Mannea, which became one of the earliest states on the territory of Azerbaijan. Historical records characterize Mannea as a neutral yet powerful state that stood against incursions of Assyria and Urartu. Unlike neighboring Media, Assyria, and Urartu, Mannea did not encroach on neighboring lands. Settlement of Cimmerian, Scythian, and Saka tribes in this country yet strengthened the positions of the Turkic people.

The downfall of the empire of Alexander the Great triggered the emergence of independent states of Atropatene and Albania on the territory of Azerbaijan. Later, in the times of historical turmoil, these polities underwent Roman and Sassanian invasions. In parallel to benefiting from Hellenism, these states sought defense from invaders. Atropatene adopted Zoroastrianism as an established faith, whereas pyrolatry dominated in the plains of Albania, and Christianity prevailed in the Albanian highland. The lands of Atropatene and Albania, which had become an arena of Sassanian-Roman wars prior to the Arab invasion, lay on the territory of the contemporary Republic of Azerbaijan. The nonaggressive nature of the politics in these two states is supported by historical records.

As a result of Arab incursions, the seventh century gave rise to common Islamic culture in Albania and Atropatene although Christianity preserved its dominant status in the Albanian mountains. Despite the fact that in AD 705 Arabs put an end to the Albanian statehood, ancient Albanians continued to remain real possessors of these lands and kept trade and cultural relations with neighbors. One of the most reliable records on the ancient Albanian history—*The History of Albania* by Moses of Kalankatuyk—provides a glimpse of that historical period. According to the writing, there were twenty-six tribes in Albania that spoke different languages and had nothing in common with Armenians. Some of the tribes spoke Turkic, and others spoke Caucasian languages. The book concludes that Armenians did not inhabit in the South Caucasus and had no neighborship with the people dwelling in this area.

The decline and dissolution of the Caliphate was followed by the emergence of independent feudal states in ninth to eleventh centuries. There are plenty of historical documents on relations between these polities and neighboring Georgians. The fact that the Shirvanshah and Shaddadi states had common borders with Georgia stipulated an abundance of historical texts that survived through ages.

Lands of Azerbaijan witnessed the rise and decline of the Eldeniz (or Eldegiz) state in the twelfth to thirteenth centuries. The Eldeniz borders ran from Georgia in the north to Central Asia in the east and Asia Minor in the west. In the fourteenth to fifteenth centuries, this vast territory was inherited by Kara-Koyunlu and Ak-Koyunlu polities. Ak-Koyunlu became the first Azerbaijani state that established formal diplomatic relations with the European states and was acknowledged as an international actor due to its immense political influence in the region. A question arises—was there any Armenian statehood in that era? It's hard to find a positive answer to this question simply because no Armenian statehood existed.

The historical legacy of Kara-Koyunlu and Ak-Koyunlu served as a ground for establishment of the Safavi state in the sixteenth century. Its territory extended from the rivers of Amu-Darya, Syr-Darya, Euphrates, and Tigris to Georgia. Originally, the official language was Azerbaijani (or Turkic). Gradually, the state evolved into the Safavi Empire and absorbed and established its rule over the neighboring territories. Yet today, Azerbaijanis don't lay any claims to other lands or fight for restoration of the Safavi Empire.

In 1722-23, the Russian emperor Peter the Great undertook the Caspian campaign. The campaign ended with seizure of the Caspian coastal territories including the city of Baku. In 1724, Peter the Great issued an edict on resettlement of Armenians on these lands. If Armenians had been populating these areas, then probably, there wouldn't be any need for such an edict. This fact reaffirms that Armenian resettlement on these territories occurred later in the history of the region.

In the mid-eighteenth century, independent khanates emerged on the territory of Azerbaijan. How could an independent Armenian state exist in this case? Even Soviet history textbooks included information on the Azerbaijani khanates in the South Caucasus.

In early nineteenth century, czarist Russia began encroachment on the South Caucasus. It is noteworthy that during its invasive march, Russia signed treaties with historical Azerbaijani territory Jar-Balaken (the Solemn Plight of 1803) and the Karabakh khanate (the Treaty of Kurekchay on May 14, 1805). The Sheki and Shirvan khanates joined the Kurekchay Treaty in May and December 1805, respectively. Here is the next question: if Armenians had existed as a political entity within the Karabakh khanate, then why aren't they mentioned in treaties between Russia and the Azerbaijani khanates? This suggests that Armenians entered the political stage in Karabakh only after the Russian invasion. The most eloquent evidence is the fifteenth clause of the Treaty of Turkmenchay signed in February 1828. This very treaty instigated resettlement of tens of thousands of Armenians from Iranian territories in the Azerbaijani lands. This fact was recorded in writings of the Russian historians V. Velichko, I. Shopen, S. Glinka, A. Griboyedov, V. Potto, N. Dubrovin, N. Shavrov, and others. In March 1828, the Russian czar Nicholas I signed an edict on establishment of an Armenian province on the territories of the invaded Erivan and Nakhchivan khanates. Following the edict, Armenians did not just undermine the relative stability in the South Caucasus but also disturbed the local demographic equilibrium.

In the late nineteenth century, Armenians from the Ottoman territories strived to obtain a home rule with the help of czarist Russia and the European states by all means, including terrorizing and killing the civil population and forming riotous groups and armed gangs. Although these events had a certain undermining effect on the Ottoman

Empire, Armenians failed to achieve their goal. Yet they continued to exploit every opportunity to demonstrate their distrust of the Ottoman state. Close to World War I, Armenians formed their troops with the blessing from the Dashnaktsutiun Party leadership and the Armenian Church and chose to fight in the war against the Ottomans. The intervention of the Russian army in Eastern Anatolia by the end of 1914 enabled the Armenians, who had been living on that territory for years, to massacre Muslim civilians. There were attempts to create an Armenian state on the Ottoman territory with the help of the Russian army; however, none of them succeeded. After failing to accomplish their objectives on the Ottoman territory, Dashnak detachments went on slaughtering Muslim population of Azerbaijan. The purpose was clear: to create an Armenian state in the South Caucasus and broaden its territory at the expense of neighboring countries.

There are plenty of documented evidences of massacres of Muslim civilians (Azerbaijani Turks) initiated by Armenian gangs in 1918-20 in the north, south, and west of Azerbaijan. Among all records, the documents of the Special Investigation Commission, compiled in 1918-20, draw particular attention. These documents constitute thirty-six volumes on 3,500 pages. These are the witness testimonies of those who survived the mass murders committed by Armenians. These documents unequivocally testify the carnage of the Azerbaijani population in 1918 in Baku, Shamakhi, Guba, and other provinces of Azerbaijan. In 1919 and 1920, the day of March 31 was commemorated by the Azerbaijani government and people as the Day of Genocide. But in 1918, the founders of the independent

Azerbaijani state who advocated peace and order in the South Caucasus, despite all the pain to make such a decision, conceded the city of Erivan, which had been the capital of the former Erivan khanate, to Armenians and allotted twenty-one seats for Armenian representatives in the first Azerbaijani parliament. Heartened by the concessions, Armenians, actively supported by Soviet Russia, seized Zangezur province of Azerbaijan and laid unjustified territorial claims to mountainous Karabakh and Nakhchivan.

Later, in early 1950s, Armenian ideologists, backed by the Soviet leadership, initiated deportation of thousands of Azerbaijanis from their homeland with the purpose to clean Armenia from Turks. Then in 1990s, the remaining Azerbaijanis were expelled from these territories and were doomed to live a refugee life. Moreover, the Armenian armed forces invaded 20 percent of the territory of the Republic of Azerbaijan, and one million people were forced to leave these lands.

Resettled in the South Caucasus in the mid-nineteenth century, Armenians brought carnage, ethnic and religious discrimination, and hatred. Today, they continue to maintain this policy.

The authors set to complete quite an uncomplicated task: to present a summary of piles of records and writings about the Armenian claims. It is up to the readers to make conclusions. We have only a rhetoric question: as opposed to Azerbaijanis, who historically advocated peace in the Caucasus and authored the idea of creation of the Caucasian House, what is the goal of the Armenians? This is the very core of the subject.

CHAPTER 1

TURKS AND ARMENIANS

1.1. The Armenian Settlement in the South Caucasus

ARMENIAN IDEOLOGISTS CLAIM that the creation of the world is allegedly attributed to Armenians. The authors of this claim opt for legends rather than historical realities. Yet actual writings about Armenians provide absolutely different insight. Herodotus, the Father of History, writes, "On the upper reaches of Euphrates lived Armenian tribes."[1] According to Tacitus, "I did not come across the name *Armenian* amongst the people abiding on the Caspian coast—Huns, Albanians, Cadusii and others."[2] The Russian historian Igor Dyakonov writes, "The Armenian ethnos was formed beyond the Caucasus."[3] Even an Armenian historian, Pastermasian, confirms, "Armenians moved to East from West in 7th-6th centuries BC."[4] According to Justin McCarthy, "The early history of the Armenians is not known with any certainty . . . It is known that . . . for many centuries Armenians remained as vassals of others, including the Roman, Persian Sassanian and Byzantine

---

[1] Herodotus, *Istoriia* [History] (Leningrad, 1972), p. 113.

[2] Tacitus Cornelius, *Sochinenia* [Writings] volume 2 (St. Petersburg, 1887), p. 395.

[3] M. M. Diakonov, *Predistoriia armianskogo naroda* [Pre-history of the Armenian people] (Yerevan, 1968), p. 93.

[4] S. S. Markosian, *Zapadnaia Armenia v kontse XIX v.* [West Armenia in late 19th century] (M., 1949), p. 322.

Empires."[5] Armenian historians feigned so many myths about the creation and formation of the Armenian people that it appears very complicated to tell facts from fiction.

The claims that Armenians have historically been living in the South Caucasus are not backed by academic researches. The actual legal document—the Kurekchay Treaty of 1805 between Russia and the Karabakh khanate—may serve as a reference to prove groundlessness of such claims. None of the eleven clauses of the treaty mentions Armenians. If Armenians indeed possessed these lands, then why did the Russian government, which broadly protected Armenians, not mention them in the treaty? Instead, the first clause expressly notes, "We, namely Khan Ibrahim of Shusha and Karabakh and Prince Pavel Tsitsianov, the Infantry General of all-Russian troops and Infantry Inspector of the Caucasian Inspection, with all authority and power endued by egregiously benign His Imperial Majesty, the most merciful and great Sovereign-Emperor Alexander Pavlovich and with God's help, concluded, resolved and signed the following conditions to initiate acceptance by Ibrahim Khan of Shusha and Karabakh, his family, kin and country, of eternal allegiance to the All-Russian Empire and its blessed sovereign Alexander Pavlovich and his exalted heirs."[6] As is evident, the treaty was

---

[5]   Justin McCarthy, Caroline McCarthy, *Turks and Armenians: A Manual on the Armenian Question* (Washington, D.C.: The Assembly of Turkish American Assosiation, 1989), p. 6.

[6]   "Traktat mezhdu Karabakhskim khanom i Rossiiskoi imperiei o perekhode khanstva pod vlast' Rossii ot 14 maia 1805 goda" ["The treaty between the Khan of Karabakh and the Russian Empire on accession of the Khanate to Russia"] (Aktı, sobranniye Kavkazkoyu Arxeograficheskoyu komissieyu [AKAK]: records

concluded with Ibrahim Khalil, the Khan of Karabakh, and testifies inherence of these lands to Azerbaijan.

It is on record that czarist Russia did not meet its commitments under the Kurekchay Treaty. In summer 1806, upon hearing of the approaching Iranian troops, Khan Ibrahim Khalil moved to Khankendi with his family (all but Mehdigulu aga). Armenians assured Major Dmitri Lisanevich that the Khan allegedly attempted to flee to Iran. Convinced by Armenians, Major Lisanevich murdered the Khan and all his family. With that, on September 10, 1806, Czar Alexander I issued a decree to appoint the son of Khan Ibrahim Khalil—Mehdigulu aga—the Khan of Karabakh. The decree read, "All rights resided in Khan Ibrahim Khalil shall pass to Khan Mehdigulu. The population shall obey the Khan, execute his orders and hold his rule in reverence."[7] Armenians are not mentioned in this edict as well. The edict signed by Emperor Alexander I is an important document that clearly identifies the real possessors of Karabakh.

DRAFT TREATY

IN THE NAME OF ALL-MIGHTY ALLAH

We, namely Khan Ibrahim of Shusha and Karabakh and Prince Pavel Tsitsianov, the Infantry General of all-Russian troops and Infantry Inspector of the Caucasian Inspection,

---

compiled by The Caucasus Archeographic Commission [RCAC]), volume 2.

[7] *Nagorniy Karabakh: sobitiia, fakty i tsyfry* [Nagorno-Karabakh: Events, facts and figures] (Baku, 2005), pp. 92-95.

with all authority and power endued by egregiously benign His Imperial Majesty the most merciful and great Sovereign-Emperor Alexander Pavlovich and with God's help, concluded, resolved and signed the following conditions to initiate acceptance by Ibrahim Khan of Shusha and Karabakh, his family, kin and country, of eternal allegiance to the All-Russian Empire and its blessed sovereign Alexander Pavlovich and his exalted heirs:

ARTICLE ONE

I, Khan Ibrahim of Shusha and Karabakh, in my own name and on behalf of my heirs and successors solemnly and everlastingly reject vassalage or any other kind of dependence of Iran or any other state, declare before the entire world that I do not accept any authority but the authority of His Imperial Majesty the Great All-Russian Sovereign-Emperor, his exalted heirs and successors, make a vow of loyalty to the throne as I am its loyal servant and shall, by tradition, take oath hereof on Holy Quran.

ARTICLE TWO

Accepting such sincere vow of His Excellency (Khan), His Imperial Majesty takes an imperial oath in his own name and on behalf of his successors that they will never refuse His Excellency Khan Ibrahim of Shusha and Karabakh and his heirs favor and benevolent auspice as his loyal citizens, in witness whereof His Imperial Majesty gives his imperial pledge to maintain the entirety of the country of His Excellency (Khan) and his successors.

ANAR ISGENDERLI

ARTICLE THREE

In return of such sincere acceptance of the supreme and only rule of All-Russian emperors and their successors by His Excellency Khan Ibrahim of Shusha and Karabakh, it is ruled that the named Khan, then his eldest son, and in this order of hereditary seniority in the genus, upon receiving an investiture through the Chief Governor of Georgia in the form of an imperial muniment granting the title of khan and confirmed by the state seal, shall solemnly give an oath of allegiance to the Russian Empire and acceptance of the supreme and only rule of the All-Russian Emperors over himself and his successors. The form of the oath is attached to the treaty, so currently governing Khan Ibrahim of Shusha and Karabakh performs this ceremony in the presence of the Chief Governor of Georgia and the executor of this ruling, the Infantry General Prince Tsitsianov.

ARTICLE FOUR

I, Khan Ibrahim of Shusha and Karabakh, in evidence of purity of my intentions and judgment and these of my successors about the allegiance to the All-Russian Empire and the acceptance of the supreme and only rule of the most serene holders of this Empire, pledge not to have relationships with adjacent rulers without prior consent of the Chief Governor of Georgia, upon arrival of their envoys or receipt of their letters of great importance, send them to the Chief Governor and request his permission, inform and seek advice about those of minor significance from the person designated by the Chief Governor of Georgia.

ARTICLE FIVE

His Imperial Majesty, graciously accepting the acknowledgment of his supreme and only rule over the dominion of His Excellency Khan Ibrahim of Shusha and Karabakh, pledges in his own name and on behalf of his successors: 1) to esteem the peoples of this dominion as his loyal subjects without any discrimination from other subjects of the vast Russian Empire; 2) to uphold invariably His Excellency Khan Ibrahim and descendants of his kin in the title of Khan of Karabakh; 3) to leave the authority over home affairs, law-court and justice, as well as revenue from the dominion at full disposal of His Excellency; 4) to assign the Russian troops of 500 men with cannons, staff and officers to Shusha fortress for protection of His Excellency and his family, as well as all his dominions, and in case of necessity of greater defense, depending on the situation and needs, the Chief Governor of Georgia shall reinforce the detachment and protect the dominions of His Excellency with the military force as territory owned by the Russian Empire.

ARTICLE SIX

I, Khan Ibrahim of Shusha and Karabakh, in sign of my faithful zeal, oblige to: 1) purvey required amount of wheat and millet grains for the aforesaid troops at a moderate price fixed by the Chief Governor of Georgia, wherefore supply of grains from Yelizavetpol shall be deemed impeded or impossible at all; 2) provide billets for the aforesaid troops in the Shusha fortress at the option of their commander, and supply them with the required amount of firewood; 3) make the entrance to Shusha fortress from the side of Yelizavetpol more convenient and carriageable for carts; 4) in case of the government's initiative to undertake laying of the road from the Shusha fortress to Javad, provide workers for this work for the price fixed by the government.

ARTICLE SEVEN

In sign of great benevolence and mercy to His Excellency Khan Ibrahim of Shusha and Karabakh, His Imperial Majesty graciously bestows upon him and his heirs a banner with the coat of arms of the Russian Empire, which shall remain with them as the sign of the title of Khan and the rule bestowed by His Imperial Majesty over the dominion and shall be taken to war, if necessary.

ARTICLE EIGHT

I, Khan Ibrahim of Shusha and Karabakh, enjoying the highest assent of His Imperial Majesty to utilize my regular revenues, pledge to contribute 8,000 gold coins annually to the treasury of His Imperial Majesty in Tiflis in two installments, with the first installment on the 1st of February and the second installment on the 1st of September, making the initial installment upon approval of the present treaty by His Imperial Majesty. In addition to all oaths of fealty, following the Asian tradition, I shall pawn the second son Shukur-Ullah of my eldest son Mammad Hasanaga to permanent residence in Tiflis.

ARTICLE NINE

His Imperial Majesty benevolently bestows daily allowance for the grandson of His Excellency, who shall reside in Tiflis, in the amount of 10 silver coins of the Russian currency.

ARTICLE TEN

This agreement is concluded in perpetuity and shall not undergo any alteration from now to eternity.

ARTICLE ELEVEN

The approval of the present treaty by a letter from His Imperial Majesty bearing the state seal shall be delivered in 6 months from signing, or earlier, if possible.

In witness thereof the underwritten parties signed these articles and affixed their seals in the camp of Yelizavetpol county, near river Kura, in summer of 1805 AD (1220 of the Islamic calendar), the 14th day of May (month of Safar).[8]

The second Russian-Persian War ended with the Treaty of Turkmenchay signed on February 10, 1828. A month later, on March 21, the Russian czar issued an edict to rename the annexed Azerbaijani khanates of Erivan and Nakhchivan to

---

[8] *Records compiled by the Caucasus Archeographic Commission,* volume 2 (Tiflis, 1868), p. 705.

the Armenian province.[9] Major General Chavchavadze, the prince of Georgia, was appointed governor of the province. Chavchavadze's daughter was married to Alexander Griboyedov, the Russian ambassador in Persia and the author of the Armenian resettlement plan.

The documents of the Caucacus Archaeography Commission implicitly show how many Armenians lived in the region prior to the Treaty of Turkmenchay: only 2,500 of total 12,000 families in the Karabakh khanate; 1,500 out of 24,000 families in the Shamakhi khanate; and 1/3 of total 15,000 families in the Shaki khanate were Armenian.[10] Catholicos Nerses Ashtaraketsi, Colonel Lazarev, and Prince Argutinski were the most fervid partisans of Armenian resettlement in the South Caucasus, especially in Erivan, Nakhchivan, and Karabakh. Another important fact is that in 1840, the Armenian province was abolished, and in 1849, the Erivan *guberniya* was created on the former territories of the Erivan and Nakhchivan khanates.[11]

The fifteenth article of the Turkmenchay Treaty regulated the resettlement of Armenians from Persian territories to the South Caucasus. Although the name *Armenian* is not worded in the treaty, the issue was agreed upon during the negotiations.

[9] *Polnoie sobranie zakonov Rossiiskoi imperii* [Complete collection of laws of the Russian Empire], collection 2, volume 3 (St. Petersburg, 1830), pp. 272-273.

[10] *Records compiled by the Caucasus Archeographic Commission*, volume 10 (Tiflis, 1885), p. 104.

[11] V. A. Potto, *Kavkazskaya voyna. Persidskaya voyna 1826-1828 gg.* [The Caucasian War. The Persian War in 1826-1828] volume 3 (Saint Petersburg, 1911; Stavropol, 2005), p. 591.

Armenians gained the most from the Treaty of Turkmenchay. By signing this treaty, the Russian czarist regime granted a homeland to thousands of Armenians scattered around the world. The edict signed by Peter I on November 10, 1724, laid the ground for Armenian relocation to the Azerbaijani lands while the treaty of 1828 further legalized this historical shift.

By the end of the seventeenth century, Armenians, failing to receive any support in Europe, sought Russian protection. In 1701, Israel Ori and Abbot Minas presented Peter I a program of thirty-six clauses, which they unsuccessfully tried to submit to European rulers. A map presented to the czar depicted lands of Erivan and Zangezur distinct from the rest of the region. In his missive to Peter I, Israel Ori wrote, "If the imperial troops of 20-30 thousand soldiers do not arrive in Shamakhi in the soonest time, we will perish and Turks will capture Erivan. Erivan is the key to the Muslim lands. Our purpose is to gain possession of Erivan. If we are able to seize Erivan, Turks and Persians will be powerless to fight against us."[12]

Jean-Baptiste Tavernier, the French writer who visited Erivan in 1655, writes in his book that the Erivan fortress was populated solely by Muslims. The French traveler Jean Chardin, who arrived in the city eighteen years later, describes the Erivan fortress as a small town in the first volume of his ten-volume collection of writings. According to him, there were eight hundred houses in the fortress, and the inhabitants were all Turks.[13]

---

[12]   T. Akopian, *İstoriya Yerevana* [The history of Yerevan] (Yerevan, 1975), p. 181.

[13]   I. Mammadov, *Tariximiz, torpağımız, taleyimiz* [Our history, land, and fate] (Baku, 2003), p. 30.

ANAR ISGENDERLI

Before the Turkmenchay Treaty, Armenian leaders, inspired by Czar Peter's edict, laid various plans on establishment of an Armenian statehood. One of the projects envisioned the establishment of a joint Armenian-Georgian state led by the Georgian king Erekle II with further submission to the Russian patronage.[14] Another draft called for establishment of an Armenian state on the Azerbaijani territories under the auspices of Prince Potemkin. These issues greatly preoccupied Empress Catherine II. In her letter to General Zubov, who commanded the invasion of Azerbaijan, she ordered, "Capture the Mugan plains and build a fortress there. May the fortress be named Yekaterinasert [Catherine's heart]. Accommodate 2 thousand Russian troops in there. Provide them with vast land plots and arms; marry them off with Armenian and Georgian girls."[15] However, Catherine's sudden death in 1796 disrupted the realization of these plans.

The Armenian historian Vardan Parsamian writes, "It is an irrefutable fact that prior to the joining of the South Caucasus to the Russian Empire Armenians did not populate these areas densely."[16]

After resettlement on the territory of North Azerbaijan, Armenians formed into a nation; and as their potentials and protection grew, they began to lay territorial claims against Azerbaijan and the Ottoman state.

---

[14] N. Dubrovin, *Zakavkaz'e v 1803-1806 godakh* [Transcaucasia in 1803-06] (St. Petersburg, 1866), p. 204.

[15] Ibid., p. 195.

[16] V. A. Parsamian, *Istoriia armianskogo naroda. 1801-1900 gg* [History of the Armenian people. 1801-1900], book 1 (Yerevan, 1977), p. 88.

If before the Turkmenchay Treaty there were 22,500 Armenians in the Erivan khanate, 2,150 Armenians in the Nakhchivan khanate, and 1,880 Armenians in the Ordubad province, the Armenian population was increased up to 669,871 by 1916.[17] In comparison, the Azerbaijani population was 313,176 in 1897 and 373,582 in 1916. According to the statistical records of 1828, 96.63 percent of lands in the Erivan khanate belonged to Azerbaijanis, and only 3.37 percent of lands were owned by Armenians.[18] In the course of the Russian-Persian War of 1826-28, 420 Azerbaijani villages were ruined within the Erivan khanate alone. In the period from 1828 to 1871, Armenians seized and appropriated 146 villages previously populated by Azerbaijanis. Chairman of the Society of Russian Patriots in Tiflis, Nikolay Shavrov, testifies, "During 1828-30 we relocated 40 thousand Armenian families from Persia and 84 thousand from the Ottoman territories to Yelizavetpol [present-day Ganja] and the most fertile lands of the Erivan *guberniya*." Shavrov further writes that besides the officially resettled population, tens of thousands of Armenian families were moved to the mountainous areas of the Yelizavetpol *guberniya* and the shores of Lake Goycha (Sevan). According to Shavrov, the total number of Armenians in the South Caucasus in early twentieth century was 1 million 300 thousand, 1 million of which were immigrants.[19]

---

[17] N. N. Shavrov, *Novaia ugroza russkomu delu v Zakavkaze. Predstoiashaia rasprodazha Mugani inorodtsam* [New threat to the Russian cause in Transcaucasia. The forthcoming sale of Mughan to aliens] (Baku, 1990), p. 42.

[18] Ibid., p. 49.

[19] Ibid., p. 93.

ANAR ISGENDERLI

The main (and undeniable) evidence, which proves the invalidity of naming the genuine Azerbaijani provinces of Erivan and Nakhchivan the Armenian province by the czarist regime in solidarity with Armenians, is that out of 107,224 people residing in these areas prior to the massive Armenian relocation from Persia and Turkey, 76.24 percent were Azerbaijanis and 23.45 percent were Armenians. The overwhelming predominance of Azerbaijanis in the ethnic composition of the local population is an evident fact that testifies that this realm historically belonged to Azerbaijanis. Mass relocations of Armenians from the Persian and Ottoman territories to these areas during and after the Russian-Persian War of 1826-28 led to a change in the ethnic balance of the population. As per the results of the official desk studies conducted in 1829-32 by Ivan Shopen, a Russian researcher of French origin, the population increased drastically and reached 164,450 people or 31,201 families in total. Around 16,100 (51.53 percent) of all registered families, or 81,749 people (49.71 percent), were Muslims (Azerbaijanis); 4,428 families (14.19 percent), or 25,151 people (15.29 percent), were Armenians who had lived in the area prior to the war; 6,949 families (22.27 percent), or 35,560 people (21.62 percent), were Armenian settlers from Persia; and 3,682 families (11.80 percent), or 21,666 people (13.17 percent), were Armenian migrants from Turkey. Thus, 57,226 Armenians (34.79 percent of the entire population of the province), or 10,631 Armenian families (34.07 percent), were officially resettled from Persia and Turkey in aggregate. The similar process was observed in the town of Erivan as well. According to the census taken after the Russian takeover of Erivan, the population of the town was composed of 1,807 Azerbaijani families (7,331 Azerbaijanis in total, with 3,749 men and 3,582 women) and 567 Armenian families, or 2,369 Armenians in total (including 1,220 men and 1149 women). Percentage-wise, the population of 9,700 people in total consisted of 75.6 percent of Azerbaijanis and 24.4 percent of Armenians.[20] As a consequence of large-scale Armenian relocations from Persia and Turkey to North Azerbaijan undertaken by the czarist regime, Armenians greatly increased in number in this town as well. As per the desk study conducted in 1829-32, 366 Armenian families, or 1,715 Armenians (903 men and 812 women), were brought from Persia, and 11 families, or 48 Armenians (25 men and 23 women), were moved from Turkey. These resettlements led to growth of the population in the town, which reached 11,463 people, and changed the ethnic balance in favor of Armenians. Thus, the Azerbaijani population decreased to 64 percent while the number of Armenians increased and reached 36 percent.[21]

In the later periods, such alterations of the populations' ethnic composition became more consistent and intentional. The edict of June 9, 1849, issued by Czar Nicholas I, established the Erivan *guberniya* on the territories of the former Armenian province and Alexandropol (Gumri) *uyezd*. The Erivan *guberniya* received a territory of 23,194.79 square *versts*

---

[20] I. Shopen, *Istoricheskii pamiatnik sostoiania Armianskoi oblasti (Erivanskoi gubernii) v epokhu prisoedinenia k Rossiiskoi imperii* [Historical memorial of the situation in the Armenian Oblast' (Erivan guberniya) in the days of accession to the Russian Empire] (St. Petersburg, 1852), p. 120.

[21] Ibid., p. 121.

(or roughly 10,191 square miles). The Caucasus Almanac of 1917 states that the population of the *guberniya* was 1,120,242 people. The population density was 48.3 heads per square verst. 589,125 (52.6 percent) of them were men and 531,117 (47.4 percent) were women; 1,014,868 (90.6 percent) were permanent residents and 105,374 (9.4 percent) were temporary residents. According to the Caucasus Almanac, despite century-long slaughters and deportations, the Azerbaijani population was 373,582 people (or 33.35 percent of the entire population). As for Armenians, their number reached 669,871 people (or 59.8 percent of the population) due to the described resettlement waves.[22]

Touching the issue of Armenian resettlement in the South Caucasus, an Armenian historian B. Ishkhanian writes, "Armenians lived in different regions of the Caucasus only in the recent centuries."[23]

The History of the 19th Century, authored by French professors Lavisse and Rambaud and translated into Russian in 1939, emphasizes that "in the middle of the 19th century Armenians were regarded as incomers to the Caucasus."[24]

In 1886, out of 326 villages in the Zangezur *uyezd* of Yelizavetpol *guberniya*, 149 were Azerbaijani, 91 were Kurdish,

---

[22] RCAC, volume 3 (Tiflis), p. 726.

[23] B. Ishkhanian, *Narodnosti Kavkaza. (Statistiko-ekonomicheskoe issledovanie)* [Ethnicities in the Caucasus. A statistical-economic reseach] (St. Petersburg, 1916), p. 16.

[24] *Istoriia XIX veka* [History of the 19th Century], edited by professors Lavisse and Rambaud. Translated from French, volume 8 (Moscow, 1939), p. 298.

and only 81 villages were Armenian.[25] By 1891, 270,400 people (or 41 percent) of the total population of 661,600 residents in Erivan *guberniya* were Azerbaijanis. In 1893, the number of Azerbaijanis was 276,000. The next census of 1897 enumerated 313,000 Azerbaijanis in the *guberniya*.

The Russian historian Sergey Glinka makes an emphasis on the merits of Colonel Lazarev, a Russian officer of Armenian descent favored by Ivan Paskevich, Count of Erivan and the commander-in-chief of the Russian troops in the Caucasus, in resettlements of Armenians to the South Caucasus, including the Azerbaijani lands. Glinka wrote, "In August 1827 Paskevich marched in Tabriz as the commander of the victorious army. In the view of the vigorous contribution of Colonel Lazarev to the matter of winning the Armenian population of Tabriz and surrounding provinces to the Russian side, Paskevich appointed him Commandant of Tabriz. Armenians, received by Lazarev, asked him to impart to His Imperial Majesty that they would be happy to live and die under his reign. Armenians from the town of Khoy came it strong and declared: 'We would rather eat Russian fodder than Persian bread.'"[26]

In his address to the Armenian population of Persia, Colonel Lazarev proclaimed, "You will receive fertile plots to be farmed at the government's expense in the places you choose—Erivan, Nakhchivan and Karabakh. You will be exempt from all kinds of duties for the following 6 years. In concord with the

---

[25] N.N. Shavrov, op. cit., p. 49.

[26] S. Glinka, *Opisanie pereseleniia armian azerbaijanskikh v peredel Rossii* [Description of the resettlement of Azerbaijani Armenians to the territory of Russia] (Moscow, 1831; Baku, 1995), p. 30.

Turkmenchay treaty, you may assign trustees in Persia to sell your property within 5 years. There [in the Azerbaijani lands] you will find a new homeland populated by Christians."[27] Lazarev, who took the lead of the Armenian resettlements, admitted himself that these lands were granted to Armenians as their new home. In his report to Count Paskevich, Colonel Lazarev wrote, "Since the 26th of February 1828—the day I took the charge, I have received 14,000 rubles in gold coins and 400,000 rubles in silver coins. For 2,000 rubles allocated for the Nakhchivan branch alone I moved 8,249 Christian families."[28]

After 1806, some 500 Azerbaijani families were driven out of the Erivan khanate and were forced to leave their motherland for Kars.[29]

As estimated by Shopen, prior to the Russian annexation of the Erivan khanate, 2,984 Azerbaijani families lived there. After the Russian invasion, the number of the Azerbaijani families in the province dropped by 3.5 times, and only 847 families remained. 2,137 Azerbaijani families were compelled to move to the neighboring Persian and Ottoman territories. By 1832, the number of Muslims in the town of Erivan dropped to 7,331 people. In 1854, only 3,163 Azerbaijanis remained in the town.[30] Alteration of the demographic situation in the South Caucasus in favor of Armenians through persuading them to resettle in Erivan and Nakhchivan provinces particularly exposed the

---

[27] Ibid., p. 48.
[28] Ibid., p. 57.
[29] RCAC, volume 7 (Tiflis, 1878), p. 86.
[30] *Kavkazskii kalendar' na 1855 g.* [The Caucasus Almanac for the year of 1955] (Tiflis, 1855), p. 341.

czarist policy to colonize the region and create a buffer zone. Immediately after the Russian-Turkish War of 1828-29, 23,098 Armenians were relocated from Persia and 20,324 from the Ottoman territory to the former Azerbaijani villages.[31]

Banishment and forced migration of Azerbaijanis in various provinces of North Azerbaijan in the first half of the nineteenth century was the direct consequence of the Russian colonization policy inculcating ethnic strives and constant conflicts. After the Russian Empire took over the Erivan khanate, 2,137 families were expelled from this province; 2,306 families from Gazakh in 1817-31; 10,334 families from Guba in 1796-1810; 11,478 families from Shamsheddin in 1804-17; 15,354 families from Borchaly in 1804-07; and 1,400 families from Nakhchivan. During 1805-13, the number of Azerbaijani families who were compelled to leave exceeded 4,840 in Karabakh alone.[32]

1.2. Armenians under the Ottoman Empire

The condition of the Armenians, who had lived long years under the Byzantine rule, was described by the Armenian historian Matthew of Edessa (Matevos Urhayetsi): "Armenians remained under oppression and yoke. The entire country broke into bloodshed."[33] Armenians were pursued for their beliefs; Armenian

---

[31]   S. Glinka, op. cit., p. 103.

[32]   V.Grigoriev, *Statisticheskoie opisanie Nakhichevanskoi provintsii* [Statistical description of Nakhchivan Province] (St. Petersburg, 1833), p. 29.

[33]   Süleyman Kocabaş, *Ermeni sorunu nedir ve ne değildir* [What is and What is not the Armenian question] (Istanbul, 1958), p. 17.

patriarchs were exiled from Byzantium. Despite all persecutions, the Armenian Church and religion managed to rescue the Armenian people and keep their cause in the agenda. After breaking away from the Roman Church, Armenians established a new patriarchy in Jerusalem in AD sixth century. In AD 993-994, the Roman army put Armenians to the sword and subdued the survivors.[34]

In quest of a refuge from the Roman threat, the Armenian Church appealed to a Seljuk sultan, Alp-Arslan, who, in return, took Armenians under his auspice and rescued them. Another sultan, Melikshah, gave an order to improve the conditions of the Armenian Church and monasteries and aid the Armenian clergy. Although Armenians, coupled with Byzantians, repeatedly levied wars against Turks, Seljuk and Ottoman rulers never interfered with their religious creed, customs, traditions, lifestyle, or national dignity. An Armenian historian Levon Dabaghian wrote, "Armenians owe to Seljuk and Ottoman Turks their current existence as a nation. If we were left to the mercy of Byzantians or other Europeans, the name 'Armenian' would be just a word in history books."[35]

The Ottoman Empire, which succeeded Seljuks, provided all conditions for Armenians to live in peace and property. After relocating the capital to Bursa, Sultan Orkhan Bey gave shelter to Armenians and let them live in Anatolia as an ethnic group. After Istanbul was conquered, the Armenian patriarchate moved there.

---

[34] Ibid., p. 24.

[35] L. Dabagian, *Voprosy istorii* [Questions of history] (Moscow, 1929), p. 22.

In the fourth decade of the seventeenth century, the Ottoman Empire was on the path of gradually losing its earlier power. A portion of Armenians entered Catholicism under pressure of the Roman Church. In 1840, the British acquired permission to build an Armenian Protestant Church in Jerusalem. In 1846, the Armenian protestant community was established in Istanbul upon British insistence. In the nineteenth century, while Gregorian, Protestant, and Catholic Armenians of Turkey whirled in religious and sectarian strives, some of the western states and czarist Russia nursed schemes for parceling the country and took solid steps to revive the Armenian chauvinism.

The Edirne Peace Treaty of 1829 between the Ottoman Empire and Russia did not fully satisfy the Russian pretensions. Nevertheless, article 14 of the peace treaty legalized resettlements of the Armenian population in the South Caucasus, including the Azerbaijani lands. Relocation of tens of thousands of Armenians from the Ottoman state to the Azerbaijani lands intrigued Russians to contemplate the establishment of West Armenia, a state within the Ottoman territory. However, the defeat in the Crimean War of 1853-56 prevented Russia from the realization of these plans. The allies of the Ottomans in the Crimean War, Great Britain and France, sought to gain influence in the region with the help of Armenians.

In March 1878, in his appeal to Sir Austen Henry Layard, the British ambassador to Istanbul, the Armenian patriarch, Nerses Varjapetian, proclaimed, "A year ago we did not have any complaints against the Ottoman governance. But the recent Russian victories have changed the situation. Now we also desire to have independent West Armenia. If you do not help, we will have to seek aid from Russians." When Layard asked where and exactly on which territories they planned to create West Armenia, the patriarch mentioned the provinces of Van, Sivas, Diyarbekir, and Cilicia. Although the British envoy adverted to the fact that Armenians did not prevail in any of those provinces, he could not overpersuade the patriarch.[36]

In April 1878, Varjapetian wrote a letter to the British foreign secretary Lord Salisbury, where he put his purpose much more explicitly: "It is no longer possible for the Armenians and the Turks to live together. Only a Christian administration can provide the equality, justice and the freedom of conscience. A Christian administration should replace the Muslim administration. Armenia (Eastern Anatolia) and Kilikya are the regions, where the Christian administration should be founded . . . This is the desire of the Armenians of Turkey."[37]

In 1877-78, the region witnessed another Russian-Turkish War. This war ended with victory of the Russians, who initiated negotiations of the truce conditions. Scattered around the world, Armenians besought Alexander II to take the so-called West Armenia from Ottomans and annex the region to Russia. The oddest aspect was that most of the letters of that kind were written and sent from within the Russian Empire—Tiflis, Ganja, Baku, and other provinces. Armenians from the Ottoman territory invoked in their letters, "As western

---

[36] Süleyman Kocabaş, op. cit., p. 59.
[37] *Zapisi grafa N. P. Ignat'eva o San-Stefano* [Notes of Count N. P. Ignatiev on San-Stefano] (St. Petersburg, 1896), p. 204.

Christians, we, Armenians, wish to gain independence with the help of Russia."[38]

Some of the clauses, which raised disputes during the peace talks between the Ottoman and Russian delegations, concerned the Armenians populating the Ottoman territories. As per Article 16 of the peace treaty, the Ottoman government was obliged to start immediate reforms in the provinces populated by Armenians and ensure their security. Article 25 implied completion of the reforms in those provinces prior to withdrawal of Russian troops within six months.[39] By Article 27, the Ottoman government vouched not to prosecute Armenians who had supported the Russian army during the war.[40] Hence, the Armenian factor became the major bargaining chip in the hands of czarist Russia, and the Western nations exploited to exert pressure on the Ottoman government. In accordance with the Treaty of San Stefano, due to inability of the Ottoman Empire to pay the imposed reparation, it was forced to withdraw from the provinces of Kars, Ardahan, Batum, Alashkerd valley, and Beyazid county in favor of Russia.[41] The czarism resolved to grant *guberniya*-level self-rule to Armenians who were close to realizing their old-time reverie of establishment of an independent state on the Ottoman territories. Nevertheless, the political jealousy of the western governments toward the provisions of the Treaty of San Stefano destroyed their plans. In fact, the European ruling regimes were not so much

---

[38] Ibid., p. 205.
[39] Ibid., p. 206.
[40] Ibid.
[41] Ibid.

disappointed with the Ottoman defeat as unwilling to put up with the growing political influence of Russia in the Balkans. This caused the calling of a conference in Berlin in summer of 1878 with participation of Austro-Hungarian, German, British, French, Italian, and Ottoman delegations. After long debates, the parties agreed to replace Armenian-related Article 16 of the San Stefano Treaty with Article 61, which implied immediate withdrawal of the Russian troops from so-called West Armenia.[42]

It is an undeniable fact, which needs to be brought to light, that Armenians had never constituted majority on the territories they inhabited. There was no Ottoman, Persian, or Russian province where the Armenians had ever exceeded one-third of the entire local population. In fact, the region had been always dominated by Turks, Kurds, and other ethnic groups.[43]

Prior to the Congress of Berlin, the Armenian delegation invoked aid from every court and cabinet in Europe. After failing to gain Italian, French, and British governments over to their cause, the Armenian delegates headed for Germany. The Congress chairman apprised Otto von Bismarck of the willingness of the Armenian delegation to receive his audience. Bismarck responded in a harsh manner: "I would not exchange a dead Pomeranian for all Armenians." Attempts of the delegation to obtain audience with the German kaiser Wilhelm I failed as well. When the head of the Armenian mission was asked which language they would speak to the Congress participants, he replied, "The language

---

[42] *Pravitel'stvenny vestnik* [The government bulletin] (St. Petersburg, 1878), p. 45.

[43] Justin McCarthy, Caroline McCarthy, op. cit., p. 18.

easily understood by everyone: by weeping and shedding tears." The Armenian mission to Europe proved futile.

Dissatisfied with such a twist of events, Armenians saw the only solution to the Armenian cause through rebellion and terror against the Ottoman state. Numerous committees, organizations, and societies—calling for the solution of the Armenian cause through violence—spawned in large cities of Europe, Asia Minor, the Caucasus, and Russia. The Hunchak and Dashnaktsutiun parties set about terrorist activities. During 1878-84, Armenians attempted two armed insurrections in Zeitun. Other armed uprisings against the Ottoman government were undertaken in Samsun (1884), Zeitun (1895), and Van (1896).[44] Despite pressures from Europe and Russia, the Ottoman government managed, although with great difficulties, to suppress the mutinies. Unable to achieve their goals in Anatolia, the Armenian gangs reached out for the South Caucasus. In pursuit of a quicker resolution of the Armenian cause under the Russian auspices, hundreds of thousands of Armenians resettled from the Ottoman provinces to the Azerbaijani territories. Consequently, the number of the Armenian population in the South Caucasus surged from 51,530 during 1812-26, when they constituted only 9.37 percent of the total population, to 784,346 in 1897.[45] According to an official

---

[44] Y. D. Lazarev, *Prichiny bedstvii armian v Turtsii* [Reasons of Armenian miseries in Turkey] (Tiflis, 1899), p. 93.

[45] A. D. Eritsov, "Dannye ob armianskom naselenii v Rossii" ["Data on the Armenian population in Russia"], *The Bulletin of The Caucasus Branch of the Imperial Russian Geographic Society*, volume 1 (Tiflis, 1881), pp. 92-93.

record, in 1829-32, the composition of the population of the Erivan and Nakhchivan provinces underwent sharp alterations under the Russian rule. A huge number of native Muslim families were forced to emigrate from these provinces to Persia and Turkey. The abandoned houses were occupied by 35,000 Armenians from Persia and 22,000 from Turkey. Here are some figures: there were 49,875 Muslims in Erivan province prior to the Russian aggression, 20,073 local Armenians, and 45,200 resettled Armenians. 17,138 Muslims and 2,690 Armenians had lived in Nakhchivan province prior to immigration of 10,670 Armenians. Ordubad district had been inhabited by 7,247 Muslims and 2,398 local Armenians, while the number of Armenian resettlers here was 1,340.[46] To put the plan into action, Armenians engaged in squeezing the local Azerbaijani population out of the native lands and bringing in Armenian immigrants. The process picked up speed at the dawn of the twentieth century. An Azerbaijani novelist Mammad Said Ordubadi wrote, "During 1905-06 Armenians ruined and razed over 200 Muslim villages in Erivan and Yelizavetpol *guberniyas* alone."[47]

Dashnaks' endeavor to create an Armenian polity from the Black Sea to the Caspian received yet wider scope on the eve of World War I. The then commander of the Third Ottoman Army

---

[46] *Grazhdanskoie upravlenie Zakavkaz'em ot prisoedineniia Gruzii do namestnichestva Velikogo Kniazia Mikhaila Nikolaevicha* [Civil governance in Transcaucasia from Georgia's accession to vicegerency of Grand Prince Mikhail Nikolayevich] (Tiflis, 1901), p. 229.

[47] M. S. Ordubadi, *Qanlı illər* [The bloody years] (Baku, 1991), p. 69.

Enver Pasha, after a meeting with Armenian leaders in Erzurum became convinced that in the event of war Armenians would take Ottomans in the rear. The reason was obvious: by giving its consent to the establishment of an Armenian autonomy on the Ottoman territories, the czarist regime managed to enlist Armenians from those areas to fight against Turks. The arrival of Czar Nicholas II in the Caucasus not long before the outbreak of World War I with a proposal to Armenians to collaborate with Russians against Ottomans yet more exacerbated the situation. The czar concluded his speech with the words, "May the ships, sailing under the Russan flag, move freely through Bosporus and Dardanelles. May the Armenian people establish an independent state on the Ottoman territory aided by the people of Russia. You shall, finally, gain liberty and justice. I believe in fidelity of Armenians, a blissful future shall come for the Armenian people. I assure you that your dreams will come true!"[48] This biased and instigating speech secured Armenian collaboration with the Russians in the war against Turkey. The Armenian troops received the blessing of the Armenian Church to prepare for invasion and depopulation of the Turkish provinces.

After the czar's address, many Armenians joined the Russian army to intrude the Ottoman provinces or sold their belongings and properties to get enlisted in voluntary Armenian detachments. Armenians were actively involved in slaughters of Turkish civilians; since Armenians were familiar with the

---

[48] Erich Feigl, *A myth of Terror. Armenian Extremism: Its Causes and Its Historical Context*, Russian edition (Baku, 2000), p. 37.

terrain, they served as guides for the Russian troops and were engaged in the organization of sabotages.[49]

On November 1, 1914, the Russian army crossed the Ottoman border in the Caucasus region. Both sides suffered heavy casualties in the battles for Kars, Ardahan, and Batum. Intervention of the Russian army in East Anatolia triggered mass killings of Turkish civilians by Armenians. The Armenians enlisted in the Russian army were joined by local Armenians to launch carnage of hundreds of thousands of civilians and oust them from their homeland. In January 1915, the Russian troops and Armenian detachments moved in Sarigamish. The next year, they occupied Erzurum in February, Isfahan in March, Trabzon in April, Khoy and Dilman in May, Arzinjan in June, and Mush in August. After plundering Muslim villages, Armenians set them on fire and sabered the population without distinction. Civilians were huddled into houses and mosques and then burned alive. Brutal aggressors buried the elderly and children alive, ripped up bellies of pregnant women to take out and strangle unborn babies, and made mothers eat the flesh of their children. In a letter addressed to the American general James G. Harbord, Kazim Karabekir Pasha wrote, "I encountered horrifying scenes in the towns we liberated. I did not see anyone alive in those towns. Children had been bayoneted. Seniors and women had been herded into basements and burned alive; juniors were hewn asunder or hung. The tragedy of my compatriots hurts to the very roots of human being."[50]

---

[49] Ibid., p. 59.

[50] Kazım Karabekir, *Erzincan ve Erzurum kurtuluşu* [Liberation of Erzinjan and Erzurum] (Ankara, 1990), p. 89.

During the war, every Armenian soldier was supplied with instructions from the Dashnaktsutiun Party. The instructions read,

> Armenians called to arms by the mobilization proclamation of the Ottoman Sultan should not succumb to the call and must prevent other people around them from joining the army.

— Armenians drafted into the army shall desert the colors by any means and join voluntary Armenian detachments;

— As soon as the Russian troops cross the border, all Armenian armed groups must join the Russian army and attack the Ottoman forces;

— All Muslims in the enemy's rear over the age of two should be murdered by all means;

— All possessions and belongings of Muslims should be seized or burned;

— Armenians should burn all houses, sowing fields, churches and charities they intend to abandon, and proclaim from pole to pole that this was done by Muslims;

— Willfully stir up the official governing circles, set ambushes and kill Ottoman officers and gendarmes;

— Murder Ottoman soldiers, who return wounded from battlefield;

— Compel civilians to leave their towns and villages;

- Arm all Armenians by producing, supplying and importing bombs and arms;
- cast the blame for Armenian-arranged sabotages and massacres on Muslims and seek publicity of the events abroad;
- perform espionage on the Ottoman territories in favor of the allied nations.[51]

The Armenian violence against the local population made the Ottoman government take defensive countermeasures. In mid-May 1915, the Armenian population of Van, Bitlis, and Erzurum was put off from combat areas and neutralized. These measures prevented Armenians from helping Russian and British troops in fighting against Ottomans. In parallel, the military command of the Ottoman government ordered Turks and other Muslims to abstain from any kind of violence against Armenians. On January 30, 1919, London-based the *Times* reported, "The Ottoman government established a special commission to deal with the issue of future return of the relocated Armenian population and with their property rights. The Commission was engaged in conducting census of the Armenian population. The papers of the Commission repeatedly mention that the Armenian population will be returned to their homes after the war."[52]

Armenian nationalists insisted that during World War I, over 1 million Armenians were killed in the Ottoman provinces.

---

[51]   J. Malevil, *Armianskaia tragedia 1915 goda* [The Armenian tragedy of 1915] (Baku, 1990), p. 40.

[52]   *Times*, January 30, 1919. See *"Armyanskiy genotsid," mif i realnost* ["Armenian genocide," myth and reality] (Baku, 1992), p. 71.

To prove this, they adduced an argument that the number of Armenians residing on the Ottoman territory prior to the war was 2.5 million. However, as per the official prewar statistics of the Ottoman government, there were 1.3 million Armenian residents on the Ottoman territory at that time. Only half of this population lived in the combat areas. During the war, half a million Armenians left Turkey for the Caucasus and other regions, 150,000-200,000 emigrated to West Europe and the United States, and some 200,000 are estimated to die of various reasons. Apart from casualties in the warfare, this figure includes those who were missing or died during relocations or of hunger and cold. In effect, the situation was completely divergent. As noted by the *Times*, "annihilation of 2 million Turks in wartime on the Ottoman territories is an undeniable truth."[53]

Armenian ideologists attempted to convince the international community that on April 24, 1915, the Ottoman minister of interior, Talat Pasha, allegedly issued a written directive legalizing the murder of Armenian population on the state level. However, these ideologists failed to produce the original document since such a paper had never existed.

A British journalist, Robert Scotland Liddell, who closely studied the events in the South Caucasus in 1918-20, writes of the Armenian propaganda: "Armenians are always in quest of fighting and present this as oppression in their propaganda. In fact, this is an earned punishment. A murdered Armenian is very valuable for Dashnaks. Such cases of murder can greatly benefit the propaganda." Scotland Liddell quotes Nuri Pasha

---

[53] Erich Feigl, op. cit., p. 57.

as a reference: "No matter when and how Armenians die, they lift up their heads from graves and cry: 'I am a victim of a mass murder.'"[54]

In 1920, the wide-scale publicity of the plans of the West European governments to split the Ottoman state coincided with publication of Aram Andonian's delusive book titled *Reminiscences of the Armenian Genocide*, which was translated into several languages. Aram Andonian claims that at the time of the British offensive on Aleppo, he met an Ottoman official, Naim Bey, from whom he received the ciphered directive of the minister of interrior, Talat Pasha, to launch massacres of Armenians. The English edition of the book includes forty-eight "official Ottoman documents" while the French translation has deviations both in content and printing of the documents. Andonian's *Reminiscences* also include fourteen photos; however, when requested, the author failed to produce the originals, claiming that he had lost them. Absence of the phrase "In the Name of Allah" in the documents' headers, which is essential for a Muslim government, and the use of the Roman calendar instead of the Muslim calendar confirm that the documents are nothing but counterfeit. Nevertheless, despite the loose ground under the book, it continues to stay in focus since it serves the interests of a number of outside actors.[55]

A thorough inspection of classified correspondence of the Ottoman leadership initiated by the Paris Peace Conference of 1919 did not find any document or order concerning an

---

[54] The State Archives of the Republic of Azerbaijan (SARA), col. 894, list 10, file 81, sheet 10.

[55] Erich Feigl, op. cit., pp. 80-81.

Armenian carnage. On the contrary, the European officials dispatched to Turkey found dozens of orders and directives issued by the Ottoman government to provide security of the relocating Armenian residents.

An American historian Stanford J. Shaw writes, "The Russian Army of the Caucasus also began an offensive towards Van with the help of a large force of Armenian volunteers . . . They reached Van on May 14 and organized and carried out a general slaughter of the local Muslim population during the next two days . . . An Armenian state was organized at Van under Russian protection. An Armenian legion was organized 'to expel the Turks from the entire southern shore of the lake in preparation for a concerted Russian drive into the Bitlis vilayet.' Thousands of Armenians from Mus and other major centers in the east began to flood into the new Armenian state, including many of those, who broke away from the deportation columns as they passed the vicinity on their way to Mosul. By mid-July there were as many as 250,000 Armenians crowded into the Van area, which before the crisis had housed and fed no more than 50,000 people, Muslim and non-Muslim alike."[56]

By mid-July 1915, Armenians committed countless crimes in these provinces. The Ottoman counteroffensive in late July pushed joint Russian-Armenian forces back; local Armenians began leaving the area together with the troops. Some 200,000 Armenians made their way toward

---

[56]   Stanford J. Shaw, *History of the Ottoman Empire and Modern Turkey*, vol. II, pp. 316-317.

the South Caucasus accompanied by the Russian army. On several occasions, the resettling Armenians were attacked by vengeance-driven Kurds who had also suffered from Armenian-initiated killings.

A more or less unbiased insight of the Armenian-Ottoman relations during and after World War I is given in *The Bristol Papers* housed in the manuscript division of the Library of the U.S. Congress. Admiral Mark Lambert Bristol served as the commander of the U.S. Naval Detachment in Turkish waters and as the U.S. high commissioner to Turkey. In this capacity, he witnessed firsthand the Turkish War of Independence and the formation of the Turkish Republic and the early years of its existence. His papers, consisting of some 33,000 items, include reports, diaries, correspondence, and copies of official dispatches, telegrams, and appointment sheets. On December 15, 1920, Bristol had a visit from Edward Fox, who provided him with additional details on the situation in Kars. In Bristol's *War Diary* for this date, the following summary of his conversation with Edward Fox, the American district commander at Kars, is given:

> The Turks marched into Kars and the Armenians ran away without firing a shot except from two or three places on the hill in the beginning, and this firing soon ceased. Many of the Armenians threw away their guns, stripped off their uniforms and hid in the houses, especially in the Near East Relief orphanages and hospitals with the children. The Turks were very badly clothed and therefore every Armenian soldier they captured they stripped and took the clothes for themselves. There were no massacres

except certain Armenians were killed and this was reported to be for crimes committed.[57]

Professor Justin McCarthy's meticulous and objective research concludes, "We now know from reliable statistics that slightly less than 600,000 Anatolian Armenians died in the wars of 1912-22, not 1.5 or 2 million, as is often claimed . . . Civil war, forced migration of both Muslims and Armenians, inter-communal warfare, disease, and, specially starvation are listed in the documents of the time as causes of death . . . The statistics tell us that 2.5 million Anatolian Muslims died as well, most of them Turks. In the Six Vilayets, the Armenian homeland, more than one million Muslims died."[58]

The above facts suggest that it was not Armenians but Turks and other Muslim population who suffered genocide during World War I in the territory of the Ottoman Empire. After failing to accomplish their ambitious plans in the Ottoman territories, the Armenian armed gangs withdrew to the South Caucasus to launch massacres of the Muslim population in the south, west, and north provinces of Azerbaijan.

---

[57] The Bristol Papers: The War Diary of the U.S. Admiral Mark Lambert Bristol, Library of the U.S. Congress.

[58] Justin McCarthy, "The Anatolian Armenians 1912-1922," *Proceedings of Symposium on Armenians in the Ottoman Empire and Turkiye (1912-1922)* (Istanbul: Bogazici University Publications, 1984), p. 23.

CHAPTER 2

FROM FEBRUARY REVOLUTION TO THE COLLAPSE OF THE TRANSCAUCASIAN SEIM

2.1. The Special Transcaucasian Committee and the Transcaucasian Commissariat

THE RUSSIAN REVOLUTION overthrew the house of Romanov, which had reigned for more than three hundred years, and paved the road for self-determination in the Southern Caucasus. The military operations between Russia and the Ottoman Empire on the Caucasus Front had an influence on the political and socioeconomical conditions in Azerbaijan, bolstered the national-democratic process, reinforced the idea of sovereignty, and, finally, strengthened the desire for independence.

Soon after the February Revolution, on March 3, the members of the Russian State *Duma* from the South Caucasus initiated the foundation of the Special Transcaucasian Committee in Tiflis. This committee included deputies from the key nations of the region. V. Kharlamov was appointed the chairman; M. Papajanov, M. Jafarov, K. Abashidze, and P. Pereverzev became the committee members.[59] The Provisional Government of Russia vested the committee with plenary powers in the South Caucasus. In fact, the Special Transcaucasian Committee started to function as an administrative body of the provisional government. However, the committee was discredited among the local population due to unequal representation and an inconsistent agrarian policy. It failed to function as a powerful state entity.

In early March 1917, the provisional government established the Executive Committee of Public Entities as its highest authority in Baku. It was composed of representatives of Councils (or Soviets) of Workers' Deputies, members of the city *duma*, and public organizations. Azerbaijanis in the executive committee were represented by Mammad Hasan Hajinski and Mammad Emin Rasulzade.[60]

Like other industrial cities of Russia, Baku also began to host Soviets of Workers' and Soldiers' Deputies. On March 7, 1917, Bolsheviks formed the Baku Soviet of Deputies consisting of fifty-two members. It is significant that there were no Azerbaijanis among the members of the Soviet.[61] Stepan Shaumian was elected the chairman of the Baku Soviet in his absence. Unlike other cities of the South Caucasus, the Soviet had a strong position in Baku.

The provisional government put the integrity of Russia in the core of its nationality program. The most influential parties—the Cadets, the Socialist-Revolutionaries, and

---

[59] The Almanac of Azerbaijan Republic for 1920, p. 8.
[60] Ibid., p. 21.
[61] Ibid., p. 23.

the Mensheviks—entrusted the resolution of ethnic self-determination issues to a Constituent Assembly, yet to be convened, and declared that they would defend the principles of ethnic-cultural autonomy. After centuries of Russian rule, the Muslim peoples of the old empire had a different agenda. The slogan National-Territorial Autonomy for Nations within Russia was proclaimed and propped by democratic forces in the All-Russian Muslim Congress held in Moscow from May 1 through May 11, 1917. One of the major issues discussed at the Congress was the future method of governance in Russia.[62]

The Musavat Party, freed to act after the February Revolution, stood out among the political forces in Azerbaijan. The Musavat backed the idea of national territorial autonomy for Azerbaijan within federative Russia and suffrage for Azerbaijani citizens from the age of twenty. In October 1917, the Musavat was strengthened by merging with the Turkic Federalist Party (Turk Edemi-Merkeziyyet). The demand for a wide national and territorial autonomy for Azerbaijan within democratic and federative Russia was one of the essential elements of the Musavat's political program.[63]

By fall 1917, the national-democratic forces increased their political influence in Azerbaijan and laid claims to establishment of a nation-state. Along with other nations under the Russian dominion, Azerbaijanis cherished hopes of realizing the dream of an independent nation-state at the Constituent Assembly.

The Bolshevik Revolution in October 1917 strengthened independent aspirations among the minority nations in Russia.

---

[62] *Caspii* newspaper issue 84 (April 16, 1917).

[63] Ibid.

The hopes for liberty were nourished by the fundamental approaches declared by Bolsheviks during their first days in power. The Decree on Peace, the Declaration of Rights of Peoples of Russia, and the Appeal to All Muslim Working Classes of Russia and the East furnished legal guarantees for the nations of the former empire to secede and establish independent states.[64] But soon, it appeared that these documents had been adopted by Bolsheviks solely for propaganda purposes and had no real implication.

In accordance with Shaumian's plot, the Baku Soviet's Executive Committee did all it could to hinder the development of democracy in Azerbaijan. For example, it kept the date of elections to the Baku Soviet secret until just before they were to be held. The goal was to prevent the increasing influence of the nationalist parties among the society and undermine their participation in the elections. Despite these hindrances, the Musavat heavily prevailed over the Socialist Revolutionaries (SR), Mensheviks, Bolsheviks, and the Armenian Dashnaks and gained an outstanding victory in the elections to Baku Soviet on October 22, 1917.[65] After the elections, the Musavat took an active part in the authority-forming process in Azerbaijan.

On November 11, 1917, the key political forces of the South Caucasus—Georgian Mensheviks, Musavat, Dashnaktsutiun, and right-wing Socialist Revolutionaries—held a meeting in

---

[64]   *Vserossiiskoe uchreditelnoe sobraniie (1917 qod v dokumentax i materialax)* [The All-Russian Constituent Assembly (1917 documents and records)] (Moscow-Leningrad, 1930), p. 54.

[65]   Almanac of Azerbaijan Republic for 1920, p. 19.

Tiflis and decided not to recognize the Bolshevik government of Russia. The parties came to an agreement to form a new Independent Transcaucasian Government (Transcaucasian Commissariat) until resolution of the authority-related issues at the All-Russian Constituent Assembly. The members of the new government were announced on November 15 in Tiflis to include D. Donskoi (Commissar on Military Affairs), Fatali Khan Khoyski (Commissar of Education), S. Alexeev-Meskhiev (Commissar of Justice), Mammad Yusif Jafarov (Commissar of Commerce and Industry), Khudat Bey Melikaslanov (Commissar of Roads and Communications), Khalil bey Khasmammadov (Commissar of State Control), A. B. Neruchev (Commissar of Agriculture), Kh. Karchikian (Commissar of Finance), A. Ohanjanian (Commissar of Public Welfare), and A. Ter-Ghazarian (Commissar of Food Supplies).[66] Georgian Menshevik E. P. Gegechkori became the head of the government. Thirty-four deputies were elected to the All-Russian Constituent Assembly from the South Caucasus, including twelve Muslims. The Transcaucasian Commissariat became a stepping-stone on the path to independence. The executive authorities of the new government proved powerless to stabilize the situation in the South Caucasus. All three nations and parties of the region formed their own national factions based on their representation in the commissariat. The Azerbaijani faction was established in late November on the initiative of M. E. Rasulzade. The decision-making process of the commissariat implied initial discussion of issues in meetings

---

[66] Ibid., p. 3.

of the factions. Only after that could final decisions be made, an essentially unworkable system.

As World War I continued and internal dissention abounded, the Transcaucasian Commissariat, ostensibly acting as an authority of the provisional government in the South Caucasus, set the preservation of the territorial integrity of the region as the foremost goal of its foreign policy. However, the commissariat's foreign policy became a bone of contention among the national factions; discord was gradually aggravated.

The place of the Transcaucasian Commissariat in the war between Ottomans and Russians was uncertain since the commissariat had no troops to defend itself. On the other hand, the factions of the commissariat had distinct views on what position to take toward the Ottoman Empire: the Muslim faction opposed fighting against the Ottomans, the Georgians considered it acceptable to come to an agreement with Turks, but the Armenians could not make any decision in this regard. In these circumstances, an opportune moment arrived for Russia, which was interested in stopping military operations in the Caucasus and looked for mediators. Eventually, on December 5, 1917, an armistice was signed between the Transcaucasian Commissariat and the Ottoman Empire in Erzincan. The terms of the armistice remained obligatory for both parties until conclusion of a peace treaty. By signing the Erzincan armistice with the Transcaucasian Commissariat and not with Soviet Russia, the Ottoman Empire indirectly recognized it as an official party. After the Erzincan truce, Russia's Caucasus Front disintegrated. Russian troops withdrew from the occupied lands of Eastern Anatolia. While retreating, the uncontrolled Russian army handed the majority of its arms over to Dashnak military units; these weapons were later used to attack Azerbaijani and Anatolia Turks.[67]

On December 19, the Transcaucasian Commissariat voted for demobilization of the Russian army in the Caucasus and formation of national troops. Armenians were first to form an army, which consisted of three infantry divisions, cavalry brigades, and territorial regiments. It was easier for Armenians and Georgians to form national armies since the Russian army had earlier incorporated many Armenian and Georgian volunteer units on the Caucasus Front. The majority of soldiers released on the Transcaucasian Front were Armenians; besides selling arms, they also joined the newly formed Armenian army. The Armenian National Council was quite well-off to buy arms in large quantities from demobilized Russian soldiers.[68]

In contrast, the Muslim National Council encountered great difficulties in attempting to form a national army. Muslims had a disadvantage compared to the Armenians and Georgians: first, there were no Azerbaijanis in the Caucasus Army. Although the 1874 general conscription was legally applied to the population of the South Caucasus in 1886, the Azerbaijanis were not drafted into the Russian army because the czarist government distrusted Muslims. Instead, in 1887

---

[67] H. Baykara, *Azərbaycan istiqlal mübarizəsi tarixi* [History of the struggle for independence of Azerbaijan] (Istanbul, 1975; reprinted: Baku, 1992), p. 58.

[68] S. E. Sef, *Kak bol'sheviki prishli k vlasti v 1917-1918 gg. v Bakinskom raione* [How Bolsheviks came to power in 1917-1918 in Baku] (Baku, 1927), p. 16.

the goverment imposed conscription of wealth on Azerbaijanis, deliberately leaving them unengaged in the military service.

The Russian army also did not have a separate Muslim unit. It was impossible to form an Azerbaijani national army based on a core of ex-Russian soldiers. The Azerbaijani political leaders, who had envisaged problems in creating an Azerbaijani army, had earlier appealed to the Provisional Government of Russia with a request for establishment of a national army. However, the appeal was denied. After the respective decision of the Transcaucasian Commissariat to create national forces, the Muslim National Council initiated gatherings of Muslim servicemen in Ganja, Baku, Lankaran, and Tiflis.

Radical actions in the process of forming of Azerbaijani national units, such as the disarming of Russian soldiers in the Shamkir railroad station in early January 1918, gave rise to anxiety among leadership of the Baku Soviet, the Armenian National Council, and certain circles of the Georgian society. However, the decision on disarmament of Russian soldiers returning from the front line had been made by the Transcaucasian Commissariat. Its decision to retain arms within the borders of the South Caucasus was approved by all three national councils. The Transcaucasian Commissariat demanded from the headquarters of the South Caucasus Front to deliver all military equipment, supplies, and weapons to the newly formed national councils. The Georgian leadership of the Transcaucasian Commissariat refused to let Russian troops enter Tiflis and suggested that they set out for Baku through Ganja and then move toward Russia. The Transcaucasian Commissariat counted on voluntary handover of arms from some of the Russian detachments moving through Azerbaijan to the members of the Muslim National Council in Shamkir and Deller railroad stations. In the beginning, the process of disarming, led by Dr. Khudadat Rafibeyov and Aslan Sefikurdski, went smoothly. After being disarmed, the soldiers were entrained and sent to Baku. However, after January 9, the troops refused to surrender their weapons. The conflict ignited from a quarrel between Georgian Abkhazava, who accompanied the troops from Tiflis, and Magalov, commander of the Muslim corps. Russian soldiers went out of control and launched fire from the trains, burning hundreds of Azerbaijani villages and killing the civilian population.

2.2. The Transcaucasian Seim

By early 1918, the Transcaucasian Commissariat had completely lost its credibility in the region and was compelled to dissolve itself. The All-Russian Constituent Assembly was to open on January 5, 1918. However, delegates from the South Caucasus were unable to travel to Russia due to closure of the roads. Soon, it became clear that Russian Bolsheviks had imposed a ban on the work of the Constituent Assembly. In these circumstances, the deputies of the assembly from the South Caucasus convened in Tiflis on February 14, 1918, to announce the establishment of the Transcaucasian Seim, which assumed the supreme authority over the region. The Seim resolved to increase the number of deputies to the Seim in accordance with the ratio of votes previously received by each party at the elections to the All-Russian Constituent Assembly. On February 23, 1918, the Transcaucasian

Seim, composed of factions led by the three major parties (Musavat, Menshevik, and Dashnaktsutiun), opened its first session. The Transcaucasian Seim included forty-four representatives of Azerbaijani political parties.[69] Unlike the Georgian and Armenian factions, the Muslim faction was marked by disunity. At a time when massacres of Turks by Dashnak-Bolshevik gangs necessitated firm measures from the Azerbaijani representatives, they proved unable to act.

Contrary to the Armenian and Georgian deputies, the Azerbaijani members of the Seim had a belligerent position toward Shaumian's Baku Soviet and fully supported the Ottoman policy in the Caucasus. On April 7, the Azerbaijani factions of the Seim except Hummet gathered to hold a comprehensive discussion of the dramatic situation in Azerbaijan. The speakers accused the government in Tiflis, composed mainly of Mensheviks, of acting in concert with Baku Bolsheviks, refusing to supply the small troop dispatched to Baku with necessary arms and ammunition and conducting secret negotiations with Vladimir Lenin. They called for immediate actions and agreed to summon a joint meeting of the Transcaucasian Seim together with other factions where they would announce the resolute position of the Muslim factions in the issue of self-determination of the Caucasus and demand resignation of Muslim ministers. Aslan Sefikurdski, leader of the Muslim Socialist Coalition, noted in his speech delivered at the Seim, "If the Transcaucasian government launched an offensive on Baku, the March massacres would not have happened. We plead with the Transcaucasian government to help us

---

[69] The Almanac of Azerbaijan Republic for 1920, p. 31.

defend ourselves and defeat bolshevism. If the Transcaucasian government exists, we demand from it to support our rightful cause. If the government does not take decisive actions against this tragedy, we will wipe them out ourselves. Our history witnessed enormous bloodshed; this page of the history will be written with blood as well."[70] Mammad Emin Rasulzade was also very critical of the government: "If from this moment on the Transcaucasian Government and Transcaucasian Seim fail to satisfy the demands of the Socialist Coalition, it would be unacceptable for us to remain calm and work together."[71] The ultimatum of the Azerbaijani delegates led to a stir in the Seim.

By the end of 1917, Germany and its allies forced Russia to retreat and abandon a part of her territory. On March 3, 1918, Soviet Russia concluded the Treaty of Brest-Litovsk with Germany and signed away West Ukrainian and West Belarusian lands in favor of Germany; Russia also agreed to withdraw from Kars, Ardahan, and Batum and cede these territories to the Ottoman Empire. By signing this treaty, Russia was forced to renounce the Decree No. 13 On the Establishment of Turkish Armenia in the territory of the Ottoman Empire, signed earlier by Lenin on January 11, 1918. On April 10, the Transcaucasian delegation declared readiness to accept the conditions of the Treaty of Brest-Litovsk and continue negotiations on this basis. But this position led to acute disputes in the Seim: The Georgian deputies insisted on mobilization of all forces to continue the war against Ottomans and appeal for Russia's help.

---

[70] SARA, col. 970, list 1, file 1, sheets 19-22.
[71] SARA, col. 970, list 1, file 1, sheets 2-24.

The Armenian faction's position was to continue the war until victory and employ all means to defeat the Ottoman State.

The Armenians shifted the blame for the retreat of the Seim forces on the Azerbaijani delegates. The Trabzon Conference between the Ottoman authorities and the Transcaucasian Seim, which had begun on March 14, was interrupted upon the Armenian and Georgian demands. At the conference, the Transcaucasian Seim attempted to add several provisions, including restoration of the Russian-Ottoman prewar borders and granting of an Armenian autonomy within the territory of the Ottoman Empire in the negotiated peace treaty. However, the leader of the Ottoman delegation, the minister of foreign affairs Husein Rauf Bey, refused to accept these conditions. Turkey insisted on the recognition of the Brest-Litovsk Peace Treaty and the immediate withdrawal from Kars, Ardahan, and Batum. The Ottomans also demanded that the Seim break away from Russia and declare independence in order to be legally recognized as a party to the negotiations.

On April 14, the Georgian and Armenian delegates interrupted the Trabzon negotiations and declared the country in a state of war with Turkey. However, the joint Armenian and Georgian forces failed to repel the attack of the Ottoman army. The next day, April 15, the Ottomans captured Batum and began to move north toward Poti. Under these circumstances, the Armenian-Georgian majority in the Seim had no choice but to declare independence of the Caucasus and fully accept the conditions of the Brest-Litovsk Treaty. Events aggravated the divisions within the Transcaucasian Seim. The Armenian, Georgian, and Azerbaijani delegates in Batum arranged separate meetings with the Ottoman mission. In the meeting with the Ottomans, the Azerbaijani delegates made fruitless attempts to talk them out of holding Batum. A Dashnak leader, Alexander Khatisov (Khatisyan), sent a representative to Rauf Bey to request a tête-à-tête meeting. As a precondition for the meeting, Khatisov demanded the return of Armenians who had left Ottoman territory and the establishment of Armenian autonomy there. In return for this concession, he offered his assistance to exert pressure on Georgians on the issue of Batum. However, Huseyn Rauf Bey rejected the proposal and refused to meet.[72] On April 22, the Seim declared establishment of the Transcaucasian Federative Democratic Republic.

The arrival of Enver Pasha, the Ottoman minister of war, in Trabzon soon after closing of the Trabzon parley turned into a remarkable event. Enver Pasha's position on the future of the South Caucasus entailed accession of the Muslim *uyezds* of Akhalkalaki and Akhalchiki to Turkey and the establishment of a federation or a confederation of Azerbaijan, Georgia, and Armenia, governed by the Transcaucasian Seim, in a close alliance with the Ottoman Empire. In case of a failure of the South Caucasian nations to unite in a federation, Enver Pasha's fallback position was to arrange an alliance between the Ottoman Empire and Azerbaijan, which had common borders with each other, on the model of Austria-Hungary.[73]

In a meeting with Enver Pasha, the member of the Seim M. H. Hajinski inquired, "What is your opinion on the

---

[72] *Dokumenty i materialy po vneshnei politike Zakavkaz'ia i Gruzii* [Documents and records on the foreign policy of Transcaucasia and Georgia] (Tbilisi, 1969), p. 86.

[73] SARA, col. 970, list 1, file 1, sheet 30.

establishment of independent Armenia?" Enver Pasha replied, "Turkey is not against an independent Armenian state, provided that Armenians abandon their intrigues against Turks in support of the British and Russian policies."[74]

Declaration of an independent Democratic Republic of the South Caucasus did not change the situation in Azerbaijan. Bolsheviks in the east and Armenian units in the west of Azerbaijan launched mass killings of the local population. The Azerbaijani delegation had great expectations of the Batum Peace Conference, to be seen below, to stop the massacres. It was clear that the only way to liberate Baku from the Bolshevik forces and put an end to Dashnak atrocities was to request help from the Ottoman Empire. In a preconference speech, the member of the Muslim faction, Nasib Yusifbeyli, gave an objective evaluation of the grave situation in Azerbaijan. Yusifbeyli contended, "In such serious circumstances we have no choice but to appeal for a foreign aid. I am the most zealous defender of our independence, but at present we should rejoice that the help comes from our friend and brother—Turkey. Our neighbors may not like this, but we have no other choice . . . We cannot cripple ourselves just to please the others. Nevertheless, we have no right to give up the idea of independence of Azerbaijan."[75]

Contentions among the three South Caucasian nations prevented unification in an independent common state. Deputies from Dashnaktsutiun officially offered a deal to the Muslim faction: they undertook to eliminate the Baku Soviet in exchange for an agreement "to keep Armenian military units

---

[74] SARA, col. 970, list 1, file 1, sheet 31.
[75] SARA, col. 970, list 1, file 1, sheet 32.

in Baku and form a multi-ethnic government in Baku rather than a purely Muslim government." The Muslim members of the Seim flatly rejected this offer and declared that the future government in Baku would remain undivided.[76] Khoyski proposed to lay the following conditions before Dashnaks: the authority in Baku should be surrendered to Azerbaijanis, Muslim military should be brought in to support the government, and the disarmed Armenian detachments should withdraw from the city. It was decided to protract the negotiations for tactical and political reasons and prevent any information leakage to Baku or the media.[77]

The talks between the Transcaucasian Republic and the Ottoman Empire resumed on the May 11, 1918, in Batum. The delegation from the South Caucasus included forty-five members and was led by the prime minister and the minister of foreign affairs Akaki Chkhenkeli. Rasulzade and Hajinski were vested with casting votes along with another four delegates. The Ottoman delegation was headed by the minister of justice, Halil Menteşe, and included, among others, the commander in chief of the Ottoman armies on the Caucasus Front, Mehmet Vehib Pasha. A German delegation led by General Otto von Lossow, the military attaché to Turkey, was present at the conference with observer status. The Turkish party initiated discussion of the draft treaty Peace and Friendship between the Ottoman Empire and the Confederative Republic of Transcaucasia. The document included some new requirements and proposals by the Ottomans that caused disagreement among the delegation

---

76 SARA, col. 970, list 1, file 1, sheet 36.
77 SARA, col. 970, list 1, file 1, sheet 38.

of the South Caucasus. The Azerbaijani delegates defended the Turkish proposals; they believed that annexation of the entire territory of Akhalkalaki and Ahyska *uyezds* and parts of Surmeli, Alexandropol, and Echmiedzin *uyezds* (where Armenians constituted a significant portion of the local population) by the Ottoman Empire would strengthen Azerbaijan's position in the South Caucasus. Appeals from the Caucasian Turks for unity under the Ottoman rule, continuing murders of Azerbaijanis by Armenians, imminence of occupation of Ganja by the Baku Soviet troops, and pro-Turkish feelings were the decisive factors for support of the Ottoman position by the Azerbaijani delegates.[78]

The political strife in the course of the Batum Conference later continued within the Transcaucasian Seim. Conflict within the Seim escalated for a number of reasons: proposals of the South Caucasian delegation were rejected by the Ottomans, whose troops were marching toward Armenia; Halil Bey Menteşe refused German mediation, and the German delegation left Batum; and the Muslim faction threatened to secede from the Seim in case of failure of the Transcaucasian government to take measures to oust Shaumian's regime from Baku.

These events signaled the approach of a crucial stage in the history of the South Caucasus. The Transcaucasian delegation, seeking a way out of the situation, shared the opinion that potentials for unification under a single government had been exhausted. Georgians, offered with the opportunity to establish

---

[78] Şahin Ergün, *Trabzon ve Batum konfransları ve anlaşmaları (1917-1918)* [Conferences and treaties of Trabzon and Batum (1917-1918)] (Ankara, 2002), p. 96.

ANAR ISGENDERLI

a unified state with the Azerbaijanis, rejected the proposal and decided to build an independent Georgian state under German protection. At the conference, the German envoys confidentially met with the Georgian delegation and promised military and economic aid. As they agreed, three thousand German troops entered the Georgian port of Poti at the time of the conference in Batum. In the meantime, on May 17, the Ottoman army pushed through and occupied Gyumri.

The Georgian faction, substantially aided by the Germans, decided to leave the Transcaucasian Federative Democratic Republic and declare independence. In these circumstances, the Muslim faction of the Seim held an extraordinary meeting on May 25, 1918, in the former Governor's Palace of Tiflis. The official statement of the faction touched upon the changes in the political situation in the South Caucasus and announced that the Georgian faction was conducting private talks in Batum and preparing to declare independence of Georgia. Besides the Azerbaijani deputies, the chairman of the Seim, Nikoloz Chkheidze, and Seim members Irakli Tsereteli and Evgeni Gegechkori were also present in the meeting. Tsereteli was first to take the floor: "The socio-democratic faction and, in general, all Georgian deputies of the Seim have come to a conclusion that the attempts to unite the nations of the South Caucasus under the slogan of independence completely failed. The fact of collapse of the Transcaucasian Government is evident. The lack of unity was clearly manifested during the negotiations with Turkey. At present, we have no another option but to declare the independence of Georgia."[79] The

---

[79]   SARA, col. 970, list 1, file 1, sheet 43[A].

chairman of the Seim, Chkheidze, expressed his deep regret for the downfall of the Seim, which was to ensure unity of the Transcaucasian nations. Khoyski replied that if this was a will of the Georgian people, then Azerbaijanis had no right to hamper it; and under these conditions, Azerbaijanis had no choice but to make the same decision.[80] After the Georgian delegation left the meeting, Khoyski stated that he had earlier spoken to Kh. Karchikian, a member of the Seim. From their conversation, it became clear that if Georgia was to declare independence, Armenia would follow the same path. After long discussions, the meeting resolved that if Georgia declared independence, Azerbaijan would declare independence as well.[81]

The complicated situation in Azerbaijan forced the national democratic forces, which were not satisfied with a role of a passive observer, to take decisive measures. Azerbaijan counted on the Ottomans to help.

The last meeting of the Transcaucasian Seim was held on May 26. The Georgian deputies left the Seim and declared independence of Georgia. The Georgian faction laid the entire blame for the dissolution of the Transcaucasian Republic upon the Muslim faction. The stance of the Georgians was that they would not work with the Muslim faction in the Seim since the latter allegedly held a pro-Turkish position. The member of Transcaucasian Seim, Shafi Rustambeyov, entirely rejecting these arguments of the Georgian faction, said, "We consider that there are no convincing and objective grounds for separation at the current difficult and responsible moment of joint political

---

[80]   SARA, col. 970, list 1, file 1, sheet 45.
[81]   SARA, col. 970, list 1, file 1, sheet 44.

existence of Transcaucasia, and factors presented by Georgian delegates are quite lame."[82]

The day after the collapse of the Transcaucasian Seim, on May 27, its Azerbaijani members held another extraordinary meeting in Tiflis to discuss the daunting situation in the region. The meeting was chaired by M. Y. Jafarov. Representatives of the Musavat, the democratic group of nonpartisans; the Muslim Socialist Block, Ittihad; the Muslim Social Democrats; and the Hummet (Mensheviks)—all former Seim members—took part in the meeting. The meeting was opened by Nasib Yusifbeyli, member of the Transcaucasian delegation in the peace negotiations with the Ottoman State in Batum. Yusifbeyli reported that the Ottomans were determined to support the independence of the Transcaucasian Republic and were ready to do their best for the strengthening, widening, and flourishing of the young statehood. He voiced the position of the Turkish delegation that unity and solidarity of the nations of the South Caucasus were the main guarantee of flourishing Transcaucasian statehood. "We have to cede some land to Armenians to achieve this goal."[83] Following Yusifbeyli's report, the meeting unanimously passed a resolution to declare the Muslim faction as an Interim National Council of Muslims of the South Caucasus. [84]

Mammad Emin Rasulzade, who was at the time in Batum holding peace talks with the Ottomans, was elected the chairman of the National Council by secret ballot; H. Aghayev

---

[82]   SARA, col. 970, list 1, file 1, sheet 45.
[83]   SARA, col. 970, list 1, file 1, sheets 46-47.
[84]   Ibid., sheet 26.

and M. Seyidov were elected vice chairmen. M. Mahmudov and R. Vekilov became secretaries of the Council. F. Khoyski was unanimously elected the chairman of the government.[85]

The meeting decided to send a delegation composed of Yusifbeyli, Shafi bey Rustambeyov, and Khosrov Pasha Sultanov from Tiflis to Ganja in order to form the Interim National Council and inform of its duties.

---

[85] Ibid., sheet 27.

CHAPTER 3

MASSACRES OF TURKS AND OTHER NATIONALITIES

THE DECLARATION OF independence in 1918 enabled Azerbaijan to investigate crimes against Turks and other Muslim population in their own homeland. One of the significant decisions of the newly formed government was the establishment of an Extraordinary Investigation Commission on June 15, 1918, to investigate crimes committed by Dashnak gangs. M. H. Hajinski, the minister of foreign affairs, noted, in his speech at the meeting of the government, that for four months, Armenian extorters had been committing atrocities against the civilian Muslim population, taking their lives and belongings. Hajinski stated that as a result of misinformation, nations of Europe had a wrong image of the ongoing processes and that these factors necessitated the establishment of a special commission. He argued that the entity should be vested with extraordinary authorities. Documents to be collected by the commission should be translated into the Azerbaijani, Russian, English, French, and German languages.[86] Lawyer Alakbar Khasmammadov was appointed the chairman of the investigation commission (later the chairman of the Azerbaijani Chamber of Appeals),

---

[86]   SARA, col. 1061, list 1, file 95, sheet 2.

Ismayil Shahmaliyev and Andrey Novatsky became members of the Ganja District Court, Nasreddin Sefikurdski was appointed the assistant public prosecutor of the Ganja District Court, and Nikolay Mikhailov and Mirza Javad Akhunzade from the Ganja Migration Office were also included in the Commission.[87]

Though the Extraordinary Investigation Commission was formed within the Ministry of Foreign Affairs, the commission was attached to the Ministry of Justice by the decision of Prime Minister Khoyski on September 22, 1918. The assistant public prosecutor of Baku District Court Alexander Kluge, the member of the grand jury Mammadkhan Tekinski, the investigator for particularly important cases of the Ganja District Court Mehiyeddin Shahmaliyev, the member of the Baku *Guberniya* District Court Hidayet Sutanov, members of the grand jury Aley Litovsky, Cheslav Klossovsky, lawyer Abbasali Haji Irzayev, and the member of Baku District Court B. Yusifbeyov sat on the commission at various times.[88]

The Extraordinary Investigation Commission exerted its best efforts to investigate grievous crimes of Dashnak gangs till April 1920. Hundreds of survivors were interrogated; numerous material evidences and photo-documents were collected.

An information sheet drawn up by a member of the commission, Klossovsky, on August 27, 1919, confirmed that the documented evidence of crimes committed by the Armenians against the Turks and other Muslims comprised thirty-six volumes on 3,500 sheets. The documents that

---

[87]   SARA, col. 1061, list 1, file 5, sheet 1.
[88]   Ibid., sheet 2.

proved the violence against the Muslim population of Baku and its suburbs filled six volumes (740 sheets in total). Four volumes (or 340 sheets) of evidence were collected on atrocities in Kurdemir and other villages of the Goychay *uyezd*, seven volumes (or 925 sheets) on the Armenian crimes in the town and *uyezd* of Shamakhi, two volumes (or 80 sheets) on the destroyed villages of the Zangezur *uyezd*, and three volumes (or 45 sheets) of documents on massacres in the town and *uyezd* of Guba.[89]

The bourgeois-democratic revolution in Russia dethroned the house of Romanov on February 17, 1917, and led to the establishment of a provisional government. The provisional government appealed to all nations of Russia and declared that with the end of the Great War, it would consider the issue of national self-determination. However, due to the Bolshevik takeover of the power in October 1917, the plan never materialized. Bolsheviks began restoration of the former empire under the ideology of the establishment of worker-peasant authority.

In late 1917 to early 1918, Baku became an arena of the open fight of Dashnak-Bolshevik groups against the Azerbaijani leaders. In December 1917, Stepan Shaumian, who was appointed an Extraordinary Commissar of the Caucasus by Vladimir Lenin, chairman of the Russian Council of People's Commissars, arrived in Baku from Tiflis together with Grigory Korganov's Military Revolutionary Committee. Shaumian was fervent in keeping soldiers, returning from the Caucasus Front, in Baku instead of sending them to Russia. All

---

[89]   SARA, col. 100, list 22, file 791, sheet 132.

these issues yet more escalated the situation in the city. Joint Bolshevik-Dashnak forces, fearing the increasing influence of the Musavat that was at the head of the Azerbaijani national movement, declared Baku the heart of the struggle between revolution and counterrevolution. The Baku Soviet, dominated by the Bolsheviks and Dashnaks, had twenty thousand troops called Red Army in its disposal.

3.1. The Massacres in Baku

The political situation in Baku was very strained in March 1918. The victory of the Musavat in the elections to the Baku Soviet seriously dismayed both Bolsheviks and Dashnaks. The Musavat came out as the most influential political party in the South Caucasus and began to struggle for the political authority and territorial sovereignty of Azerbaijan. Bolsheviks, under the leadership of Shaumian and together with the leaders of the Armenian National Council and the Dashnaktsutiun, launched a hostile campaign against the Musavat. Shaumian obtained information on the poorly armed and outnumbered Azerbaijani national movement in Baku and commenced preparations for a massacre "to teach a lesson to the Muslims."

On March 29, 1918, Bolsheviks disarmed a small Muslim crew onboard the steamship *Evelina* in Baku; the incident was exploited to start an ethnic massacre against Azerbaijanis.

Earlier that month, on March 17, a small group from the Muslim Division—forty-eight servicemen—had brought the body of Mahammad Taghiyev (son of an oil baron, Haji Zeynalabdin Taghiyev), who died from negligent handling of a weapon, to Baku. The arrival of the armed soldiers caused a stir among the Bolsheviks. The group was planning to return to Lankaran on the *Evelina* after the funeral. Upon departure of the steamship, it was held back by the armed Bolsheviks who requested everyone onboard to disarm. When the soldiers onboard refused to surrender, the Bolsheviks fired rifles and machine guns on the vessel. The incident ended with the disarming of the Azerbaijani servicemen by the Bolsheviks.

The next day, on March 31, at four in the afternoon, a delegation from several Azerbaijani parties appeared before the Executive Committee of the Soviet and asked for arms for the Muslims. Prokofy Japaridze, the chairman of the Executive Committee of the Baku Soviet, asked if this request could be considered an ultimatum, and the delegation declared that they had no other interest than to cool the passions of the Azerbaijani masses. Japaridze assured the Muslim leaders that he would take the matter to the Military-Revolutionary Committee of the Caucasian Army and support the granting of arms to the Muslims.[90]

The following day, Armenian soldiers appeared in the southern part of the city. They began digging trenches and erecting barricades from sand and stones. The same day, the former mayor of Baku, Ter-Mikaelian, came to the meeting of Azerbaijani parties held in the building of the Muslim Charity and declared on behalf of the Armenian National Council and the Dashnaktsutiun Party that in case of a Muslim uprising against the Bolsheviks, Armenians would join Azerbaijanis in dislodging the Bolsheviks from the city. Yet on March 31, early

---

[90]   Ronald Grigor Suny, *The Baku Commune, 1917-1918: Class and Nationality in the Russian Revolution*, p. 217.

in the morning, the Muslim quarters of the city underwent attacks. The Muslims had been betrayed by the Armenian leaders. On the eve of the carnage, all Armenians who lived in the Muslim neighborhoods had moved to the Armenian quarters of the city. However, other Christian residents, namely Russians and Georgians, stayed in the Muslim quarters.

The slaughters in Baku had been elaborated by the Dashnaktsutiun and the Armenian National Council at the end of 1917. The Armenian leadership made repeated attempts to instigate Azerbaijanis to an armed confrontation with Bolsheviks; the goal was to physically annihilate the Muslim population. Killings and wrecking in the Muslim quarters were committed by the organized Armenian military units in a prearranged and coordinated manner. On January 6-9, 1918, Azerbaijani troops disarmed Russian detachments returning from the Caucasus Front at Shamkir railroad station near Ganja. Despite the fact that the Azerbaijani troops were guided by a special directive of the Transcaucasian Commissariat, the detachment commanders refused to surrender their weapons under the influence of Bolshevik propaganda. The confrontation escalated to a clash of arms with dead and injured on both sides. The incident was utilized by Shaumian, who laid the entire guilt on the Azerbaijani troops and attempted a mass slaughter. However, he was forced to forgo the idea in the view of unfavourable balance of forces.

In the early evening of March 31, a Revolutionary Defense Committee was formed to coordinate the operations against the Azerbaijanis. The committee's membership included Shaumian, Japaridze, Korganov, Sukhartsev, Sahakian, Melik-Eolchian, and Dr. Narimanov. In its first proclamation, the committee declared itself "the highest military-political organ" in Baku, accountable only to the Soviet.[91] As soon as the conflict between the Soviet forces and the Muslims began, the Armenian community declared its neutral position in this confrontation. Clearly, the side that could win the Armenian military units over to its cause would have the preponderance of strength and could be assured of victory.[92] Tactically, the Dashnaktsutiun Party and the Armenian National Council rejected alliance with the Musavat. The Armenian National Council held negotiations with the Soviet leaders and drew their forces to the Armenian quarters of the city.

Involvement of the Armenian military units initiated by Shaumian, the head of the Baku Soviet, yet more widened the scope of the massacre. Under the pretext of protection of the Bolsheviks, Armenian military units began to slaughter the Azerbaijani population. It is noteworthy that both the Baku Soviet troops consisted of Armenians. The Dashnaks in the Soviet, Sako Sahakian, Arakelian, and others flatly opposed the admittance of Muslim workers to the Bolshevik detachments. While they prevented the Azerbaijanis from forming a national army, the Dashnaks conducted their Armenian nationalist policy under the veil of the Soviet ideology and prepared for massacres against the Azerbaijani population of Baku, Shamakhi, and other provinces of Azerbaijan. The Armenian National Council had a special role in these atrocities. The February Revolution of 1917 enabled Armenian political organizations to establish Armenian National Councils driven with anti-Azerbaijani

---

[91]   *Izvestiia*, no. 64 (286) (April 2, 1918); cited in Suny, op. cit., p. 218.

[92]   Arev, no. 63 (April 10, 1918); cited in Suny, op. cit., p. 218.

agenda in Baku, Ganja, Shusha, Nakhchivan, Julfa, Ordubad, and Zangezur. These councils were utilized as a political tool to propagandize and mobilize the Armenian population.

The right wing of the Armenian National Council in Baku published a twice-weekly newspaper *Nashe Vremya* with financial support of the Armenian bourgeois class. The newspaper was notable for its extreme chauvinistic position, slanderous and subversive campaigns against the Muslim population, and justifying the crimes committed by the Dashnak gangs.

In early March 1918, the Armenian National Council in Baku issued an appeal "to Armenian fighters" where it called the zinvors (i.e., members of Armenian terrorist groups) for armed struggle against the "eternal foe," referring to Turkic population.

When the ethnic conflict ignited in Baku, the Armenian National Council initially announced its neutrality and noninvolvement. However, when the situation changed in favor of the Baku Soviet, the council transferred its troops at the command of the Revolutionary Defense Committee. Azerbaijanis underwent attacks and lootings in Shamakhi, Goychay, Ganja, Nukha, Gazakh, Lankaran, Salyan—in short, in all provinces of Azerbaijan.

A. N. Kvasnik, a Jewish resident of Baku and an eyewitness of the events, testified during interrogation by the Investigation Committee: "The events in Baku on March 17 through March 21 [by Julian calendar] of this year can be described with a quiet conscience as a violent attempt upon Muslims committed by Armenians with the purpose to annihilate Muslims first of all in Baku, and then in other places, to loot their properties and to seize their belongings."[93]

---

[93]   SARA, col. 1061, list 1, file 95, sheet 2.

The unbridled and savage Armenian gangs used the most brutal methods to kill Azerbaijani civilians. Alexander Kluge, member of the Extraordinary Investigation Commission, wrote in a report titled "On the Case of Violence against the Muslim Population of Baku," "Well-armed and trained Armenian soldiers attacked using numerous machine-guns . . . Armenians were braking in the Muslims' houses, killing and cutting them into pieces by swords and daggers, stabbing with bayonets, throwing children into burning houses, ruthlessly tossing up infants, whose parents had been already murdered, on the tips of bayonets; they killed all." Besides killing the Muslims, the Armenian bashers ruined their properties and carried away valuable belongings.[94] Later, fifty-seven corpses of Muslim women and girls were found commonly buried at one site alone; their ears and noses were cut, and abdomens were torn. When the Armenians had no time to kill women, they tied them to one another by their braided hair and carried them away on carts, crippling the women by beating them with the butts of their rifles.[95]

Based on the documents of the investigation commission, approximately eleven thousand Azerbaijanis were killed in Baku in March of 1918. Bodies of many people were missing; according to witnesses' testimonies, Armenians threw corpses into burning houses, the sea, and wells to cover up the crimes.[96]

---

[94] State Archive on Political Parties and Public Movements of the Republic of Azerbaijan (SAPPPMRA), col.277, list 2, file 16, sheet 20.

[95] Ibid., sheet 18.

[96] Ibid., sheet 18.

Jewelry and possessions to the tune of four hundred million rubles were confiscated from the Azerbaijani population of Baku. Many shrines and historical sites were ruined. The Tezepir Mosque was damaged by long-range shellfire. The Ismailiyye Building, one of the finest examples of Muslim architecture in the city, was burnt down.[97]

This barbarism is described in the papers of the investigation commission: "On March 18, 1918 [by the Julian calendar] an Armenian officer with three Armenian soldiers entered the building of the Ismailiyye Muslim Charity from the blind alley between the building and the editorial office of *Kaspii*. Soon fire and smoke appeared in the windows of the building. Ismailiyye, the pride of Baku Muslims and one of the most charming landmarks of the city, was destroyed by fire. There was nobody to put out the fire, because Muslims could not leave their houses due to the risk to be killed by machine-gun fire."[98] That officer responsible was a notorious leader of the Dashnaktsutiun Party, Tatevos Amirov.

Looters burned the buildings of the editorial office of *Kaspii*, the Dagestan hotel, and the Iskenderiyye and Ismailiyye buildings.[99] Azerbaijanis were not the only people that were massacred; other Muslims of the Caucasus were abused as well. The Baku Muslim Charity and the Caucasus Muslim Committees were headquartered in the Ismailiyye building; all their funds and documents were kept there, and the building was also utilized as the place for meetings and assemblies

---

[97] Ibid., files 13-16, sheets 25-26.

[98] Ibid.

[99] Ibid., sheet 18.

of Muslims. The editorial office of *Kaspii*, besides its main function, also published books in the Azerbaijani language. Five thousand copies of the Quran had been kept in the building prior to the fire; they were burned to ashes along with the building.[100]

Armenian intellectuals and youth were engaged in the March massacres side by side with the well-trained military units. This is witnessed in the documents compiled during the investigation: "Representatives of all classes of the Armenian people felt obliged to take part in this 'war.' Engineers, doctors, and clerks were among them; in short, all strata of the Armenian society were performing their 'civic duty.'"[101]

On March 24, ten armed sailors, led by the pilot Rozenblum, were sent to Kazim Akhundov, the second in command of the steamship *Nikolai Buniatov*, to solicit protection of the hillside quarters of Baku—Chenberekend. The next day, on March 25, Akhundov ordered the sailors to collect corpses from the Nikolayevskaya Street. They alone collected the bodies of 3 Muslim schoolboys and 11 schoolgirls, 1 Russian woman and 8 Russian men, 3 Muslim boys aged three to five, 19 female Persian nationals, and 67 Azerbaijanis of various trades who had been slaughtered with swords or stabbed with bayonets. In addition, 6,748 corpses of Azerbaijani men, women, and children were brought to the old quay of the Vulkan Company.[102] Akhundov testified that he took his comrade, fitter Vladimir Sokolov, to a brickyard (*Kerpich-khana*) where they took three photos. The

---

[100] SARA, col.100, list 3, file 91, sheet 7.
[101] SARA, col.100, list 2, file 650, sheets 9-10.
[102] SAPPPMRA, col.277, list 3, file 15, sheet 20.

first photo was of a female corpse: the woman had a bullet wound on the head, five bayonet wounds on the body, and a sword wound on the right collarbone. There was a child on her right breast, still alive. The infant, who was trying to suck his mother, had a bayonet wound on the leg. In the second photo, a two-year-old child was nailed to the wall. It is clearly seen from the nail head that it had been hammered into the boy with a stone left nearby. The third photo was of the corpse of a teenage girl with clear marks of a group rape.[103] At the entrance of the fourth house, Akhundov and Sokolov encountered a terrible sight: on the floor of a large room, there were corpses of a twenty-two- to twenty-three-year-old woman, two elderly women, a girl and a boy aged eight or nine, and an infant. The infant's limbs had been chewed by dogs. Sokolov, deeply troubled by the scene, was not able to take any photos.[104]

Looters had no pity even for the people they personally knew. For example, on March 20, Stepan Lalayev, with a group of Armenian soldiers, broke into the house of Dr. Beybala Sultanov and killed him with a handgun. Then Lalayev went down to the yard and shot a Muslim yard keeper, his wife, and his two-year-old son. A group of some thirty armed Armenians broke into the apartment of Mashadi Ahmed Rahim-Oghlu and took away valuables in the amount of 34,840 rubles. Mashadi Ahmed identified his neighbors—tailor Hayk and shopkeeper Yekhush—among the criminals.[105]

---

[103] SARA, col.100, list 3, file 16, sheet 14.
[104] Ibid., sheet 15.
[105] SARA, col.100, list 4, file 10, sheet 4.

The tragic events in Baku caused serious damage to the city. The outbreak of an epidemic killed thousands of people, and water and food supplies were interrupted. Grocery stores and bazaars were empty. All the remaining food was taken away by looters. Press headlines—Population Suffers from Hunger—clearly depicted the situation.[106]

The first book on the 1918 massacres of Azerbaijanis was written by Mahammad Muradzade and published in 1919 in Baku.[107] Muradzade himself was an eyewitness and a survivor of Armenian savageries. The author described the massacres, using his family as an example, and gave a clear picture of Armenian vandalism and ferocity in Baku and in provinces of Azerbaijan. The author writes, "A heartbreaking scene, which I witnessed, still continues to arise in my mind. That day I saw several men carrying a short ladder on their shoulders with a corpse wrapped in a colorful carpet. That corpse was my poor father's—the figurative victim of the March days. During those days even this sight was envied by many. The bodies of many martyrs were missing after the massacre. Mothers and sisters were bitterly grieving. That day more than half of Baku was mourning. Many families were slaughtered with poisoned daggers without mercy even for infants. There was no house where cry and wail were not heard."[108]

The population of the cul-de-sac, a typical street in the Muslim quarters where the author lived, turned to Jews for

---

[106] Ibid., sheet 3.
[107] M. Muradzade, *Mart Hadise-I elimesi* [The March events] (Baku, 1919; 1996).
[108] Ibid., pp.27-29.

help. As a matter of fact, the Jewish population gave a helping hand and saved the lives of thousands of Muslims during the massacre in Baku. The majority of witnesses who testified before the investigation committee were Jews. The author, sheltered by a Jewish family by his father's request, gives the following description of the events: "It was nearly one o'clock. A clatter and then several shots sounded on the roof. At this point I saw my younger brother running towards us and shouting. Suddenly someone furiously knocked at the door and windows, and then I heard several rifle-shots. My father's voice no longer came through."[109] The Dashnak detachments besieged the Muslim quarter and began to slaughter the population without any distinction. Not only men but also women were taken hostage. By doing this, the Dashnaks openly expressed hatred toward Azerbaijanis: "The thugs led away two female hostages like an animal flock. Then the other mobsters ransacked and looted the houses and the yards. They questioned the Jews about the Muslim abodes and attempted to enter into the house. The Jews refused to let them in and said the house belonged to them and there were no Muslims inside; they said that Muslims had lived next door, pointing at our house, but all of them had been killed an hour ago. Our abandoned house, which had already been looted once, was plundered again by these gangsters."[110] Besides slaughtering Muslims, the Dashnak-Bolshevik gangs herded those whom they had not been able to kill into public buildings and abused them.

---

[109] Ibid., p. 16.
[110] Ibid., pp. 20-21.

ANAR ISGENDERLI

According to the author, on the third day of the massacre, Jewish children began to scurry through the quarters to find out who was still alive. When they returned, they described what they had seen. News spread that "martyrs lied in bloody deathbeds, scattered along streets like fish dumped on the shore. Vampires of the neighboring nation [Armenians] searched, found and killed Turkic-Muslim children, who had been hiding in nooks. They intruded into Russian and Jewish dwellings and forced the inhabitants to surrender Muslims on pain of death."[111] The author has a description of the role of the Jewish youth in sheltering of Azerbaijanis: "Several Jewish youngsters, formerly enlisted in the old Russian army, took up arms and claimed that there were no Muslims in the neighborhood and that they had been appointed by the commander to defend several houses from criminal intrusion; they kept alert against any infringement. These young men defended their families from assaults and rescued us from the arms of death."[112]

The Bolshevik-Dashnak alliance led by Shaumian claimed that the total death toll during the March events was only three thousand. According to Muradzade, all streets of Baku were packed with bodies: "Rumble of carts, rushing to clean the streets from countless corpses after the 2-day war, set the city in anxiety."[113]

After the Bolshevik invasion in 1920, not only was this tragedy forgotten, but it was also described as a civil war where nationalists were viewed as the main culprits of the hostilities.

---

[111] Ibid., p. 23.
[112] Ibid.
[113] Ibid., p. 24.

Shaumian and other bloodthirsty authors of the massacre were proclaimed national heroes; the central streets of Baku, where the majority of Azerbaijanis had been slaughtered, were named in the honor of these criminals.

Another eyewitness of the events, Boris Baikov, who lived in Baku from 1895 to 1919 prior to emigrating to Berlin, described the March massacres in his *Memories of the Revolution in Transcaucasia*. In his book, Baikov expressed his position on the situation in the South Caucasus prior to the March events and wrote that the collapse of czarism in February 1917 cleared the way for independence of the South Caucasian nations. At that time, Armenians, Georgians, and Azerbaijanis sought self-rule within the borders of Russia. On the other hand, every political force in Russia had its own distinct view on the problem of independence of these nations. The Bolsheviks' declaration on granting rights to nations for their self-determination remained only a slogan. In reality, the Bolsheviks struggled to preserve the former Russian borders and fill them with a new content. The October Revolution cleared all doubts and confirmed the Bolsheviks' intentions. Baikov wrote, "The entire oil [supply] in Czarist Russia was supplied from Baku. The main bulk of the oil was forwarded by sea and through the Volga River to the Russian cities. Trade ships resumed operations in the middle of March, when it began thawing. The Bolsheviks' primary concern was to occupy Baku in the short run."[114]

The author continued, "The Bolsheviks did not keep back their intentions. They began to accumulate military units and arms from Transcaucasia in one place. The Caspian Fleet

---

[114] Baikov, op. cit., p. 119.

ANAR ISGENDERLI

was controlled by the Bolsheviks."[115] Baikov argued that the Bolsheviks possessed enough force to seize power in Baku, but this task would be hampered if Dashnaks joined forces with the Musavat. However, the Bolsheviks were sure that the Dashnaks would not support the Musavat on the issue of power. Baikov writes, "The sitting of the city *Duma* was held on March 24, in the evening. At 7 p.m. the meeting was disrupted by the news that the Bolsheviks' attempt to disarm the steamship *Evelina* at its departure for Lankaran led to a skirmish. At 11 p.m. the Muslim troops on the ship surrendered their arms to the Bolsheviks."[116]

A few days before the massacre, the Armenian National Council officially declared that in case of a conflict between Muslims and Bolsheviks, Armenians would maintain neutrality. But on the next day, when Bolsheviks refused to return the arms to Muslims, the dubious behavior of the Armenians gave rise to a concern. The author wrote, "I lived in the downtown, therefore no action escaped my notice. On March 24 at 4 p.m. the Bolsheviks and the Musavatists began negotiations on return of arms. We thought that the talks took a normal course. But an hour later, at 5 p.m., the Muslim quarters on the hill-side underwent shell-fire from the sea. Terrible fights started in the city."[117] As the author describes, "The city went through hell during those four days. On the first day the Muslims overpowered [their attackers], but on the next day, the Bolsheviks outbalanced them and began an unequal battle."

---

[115] Ibid., p. 120.
[116] Ibid.
[117] Ibid., p. 122.

Baikov emphasizes the critical moment in the fighting: "The Armenian National Council tried to protect the Armenian population from the battle. But the Dashnaktsutiun Party rendered a decision on engagement of the Armenian troops on the Bolsheviks' side. On the second day the course of the battles changed and the majority of Armenians began to fight against Muslims."[118]

According to the author, there was a confrontation between the Armenian National Council and the Dashnaktsutiun Party on the issue of involvement in the massacre. Except Baikov, none of the authors who wrote on the subject paid attention to this issue. The author described the hostilities: "Fire was everywhere. Artillery of the Bolsheviks reduced the city to the ruins. The Juma mosque was damaged, the Ismailiyya building was set on fire, the printing house of the *Kaspii* newspaper was destroyed. The Muslims fled the city en masse. The helpless Muslims left their homes and tried to hide in back streets and alleys to stay alive. But none of them could survive the shell-fire."[119]

Baikov brought further facts not described by other authors: "The crimes against the Muslim population had a great influence on the personnel of the two Russian infantry regiments [at that time deployed in Baku], which numbered roughly 8,000. The Bolsheviks kept these regiments in Baku by force. The regiment commander demanded from Shaumian and other Bolsheviks to stop fighting that day [on April 1], otherwise they threatened to engage on the Muslims' side.

---

[118] Ibid.
[119] Ibid., p. 121.

The Bolsheviks were compelled to stop hostilities after this demand."[120]

Baikov did not disclose his thoughts in regard to Shaumian's Bolshevik government formed after the massacre but noted that a warrant officer, Avakian, appointed the city commandant, was a drug addict and mentally deviant. According to Soviet historians S. Sef and Y. Ratgauzer, Avakian demonstrated particular brutality toward the Muslim population of Baku, confiscated property of well-to-do townsmen, and spent day after day in drunkenness.[121]

Another appealing account of the March days is given by a French historian, Henry Barby.[122] According to Barby, "7,000 Muslims and 3,000 Bolsheviks and Armenians were killed in the March massacre of 1918."[123] Although his death toll for Muslims is not fully accurate, it only slightly deviates from the real figures. From Barby's description of the subsequent events, it is seen that the author had done quite an extensive research on the subject: "The Bolshevik leaders Shaumian, Fioletov, Japaridze were arrested [in late July to early August 1918]. 80 million rubles in gold coins were found on the ship among Shaumian's luggage."[124]

---

[120] Ibid.

[121] S. E. Sef, *Bor'ba za Oktyabr v Baku* [Struggle for October in Baku] (Tbilisi, 1930)

Y. Ratgauzer, *Revolutsiya i grazhdanskaya voina v Baku* [The revolution and civil war in Baku. Part One. 1917-1918] (Baku, 1927).

[122] Henry Barby, *Le debacle russe: les extravagances Bolcheviques et l'epopee Armenienne* (Paris, 1921).

[123] Ibid., p. 65.

[124] Ibid., p. 94.

An American historian, Firuz Kazemzadeh, also conducted a comprehensive study on the 1918 genocide of Azerbaijanis. The 345-page work published in 1951[125] is distinguished by an abundance of sources.

Kazemzadeh looked predominantly into the essence of the tragedy and wrote that no matter who started shooting first, it was the biggest tragedy of the period. At the time of publication of the book, Soviet historians claimed that there had been a civil war in Baku in 1918 but avoided to give any figures on human losses. They refused to confess that thousands of elderly, youth, and children had undergone fiendish tortures and been murdered.

In the chapter devoted to the massacres of Muslims in Baku, the author writes, "On 9th March, 1918, there arrived in Baku the staff of the Azerbaijani Savage Division. Its Commander, General Taleshinskii, was arrested by the Soviet. The Muslim masses were excited. Meetings were held in the mosques, in which orators called on the people to offer armed resistance to the Soviet. Shaumian could have prevented much bloodshed, had he been less impulsive and stubborn. Only a few days before the arrival of General Taleshinskii and his staff, he had received a telegram from Lenin . . . The telegram shows that Lenin, with his genius for appreciating people, felt the rashness of Shaumian. Lenin's advice about diplomacy was nothing but a warning to be more careful and less provoking."[126]

---

[125] F. Kazemzadeh, *The Struggle for Transcaucasia (1917-1921)* (New York, 1951).

[126] F. Kazemzadeh, op. cit., p. 67.

According to Kazemzadeh, the release of Talyshinski might have closed the incident. Kazemzadeh describes the situation in Baku on the eve of the events: "Trenches were being dug, barricades erected, and preparations made for real warfare. For a few hours the city was quiet, as nature often is before a storm. When the Soviet realized that a fully fledged civil war was approaching, it looked around for allies, knowing full well that its own forces were insufficient against the Azerbaijani masses led by the Musavat."[127] Suny, Swietochowski, Baikov, and other foreign historians argued that without alliance, the Soviet would certainly lose in the confrontation with the Musavat, which, at that time, enjoyed wide popular support. The leader of the Baku Mensheviks, Aiollo, declared that they would support the Soviet. The SRs pledged themselves to fight against Pan-Islamism and the "socialists a l'orientale." Even the Cadets (right-wing liberals) promised to support the Bolsheviks as the champions of the "Russian cause."[128] Therein, the plans of the Dashnaktsutiun Party and the Bolsheviks complemented each other.

Kazemzadeh continues, "In that bloodthirsty episode, which had such fatal effects upon the Muslims, the principal part was played by the Armenians, who were then in Baku, clustering as elsewhere around their nationalist party [Dashnaktsutiun] . . . The truth is that the Armenians, under the guise of Bolshevism, rushed on the Muslims and massacred during a few frightful days more than twelve thousand people, many of whom were old men, women, and children."[129]

---

[127] Ibid., p. 71.
[128] Baikov, op. cit., p. 122. Cited in F. Kazemzadeh, op. cit., p. 72.
[129] F. Kazemzadeh, op. cit. p.73.

As confirmed also by the evidences collected by the Extraordinary Investigation Commission, "the March Events, as this episode became known to history, touched off a series of massacres all over Azerbaijan. The brutalities continued for weeks. No quarter was given by either side: neither age nor sex was respected. Enormous crowds roamed the streets, burning houses, killing every passer-by who was identified as an enemy; many innocent persons suffering death at the hands of both the Armenians and the Azerbaijanis. The struggle which had begun as a political contest between the Musavat and the Soviet assumed the character of a gigantic race riot."[130]

After the massacre, all parties tried to justify themselves. The Armenian archbishop Bagrat denied involvement of Armenians in the March incidents in the document presented to General Harbord, the head of a U.S. delegation (the American Military Missions to Armenia, known as the Harbord Commission) that visited Baku in fall 1919. Bagrat eclipsed Shaumian, claiming that three hundred Armenians and only seven hundred Muslims were killed during the massacres in Baku. "Bagrat stated that the battle was waged by the Musavat and the Soviet, while the Armenians remained neutral. It is true, he continued, that some Armenian soldiers took part in the fighting, but those were only isolated individuals for whom the Armenian National Council could not be held responsible. The Archbishop placed the entire guilt upon the Musavat, which, according to the letter, was a helper of the Turks."[131]

---

[130] SARA, col.100, list 3, file 791, sheet 8; F. Kazemzadeh, op. cit. p.73.

[131] F. Kazemzadeh, op. cit. p.82.

Seyid Jafar Pishavari, the chairman of the 1945-46 National Government of South Azerbaijan and an eyewitness of the clashes, wrote in his memoirs, "I saw the savageries of the Dashnaks, who killed and burned many innocent people, and especially neutral South Azerbaijanis in the caravanserais on March 18, 1918 [Julian calendar]. The crimes, committed by the Dashnaks without any reason and only because of spite and hatred, distressed everyone. All streets, shops, houses—the entire city was in blood and had been looted. The Armenians murdered Azerbaijani Turks and took women as prisoners."[132]

After getting hold of absolute power in Baku and a number of *uyezds*, the Bolsheviks started the process of general nationalization to strengthen their positions. The Bolsheviks achieved integration of the Armenian troops to avoid confrontation with the Armenian National Council and the Dashnaktsutiun Party. On the other hand, the Armenian leaders, exhausted in the struggle with the Musavat and fearing the approach of the Ottoman forces, agreed to incorporate their forces into the Red Army. The Armenians, thus united by the Soviets, guaranteed their claim for power and prepared for further linkage with Andranik's detachments banished from the Ottoman territory. On April 25, 1918, the Bolsheviks formed the Baku Soviet of People's Commissars to formalize the monopoly of power. The Soviet was composed of the Bolsheviks and their supporters and declared itself the single authority over the entire region of Baku and its population of one million. The Baku Soviet spent a portion of the fifty million manats

---

[132] S. J. Pishavari, *Seçilmiş əsərləri* [Selected works] (Baku, 1965), pp. 297-298.

that had been extorted from local tycoons for development of the oil industry. During the period in power from April 25 to July 31, 1918, the Bolsheviks arranged shipping of tons of oil from Baku to Russia.

The period of the Azerbaijani history between 1917 and 1920 was researched by another American historian, Ronald Grigor Suny. His book, *The Baku Commune 1917-1918*,[133] provides a comprehensive insight into the March events.

The author describes the Dashnaktsutiun politics prior to the March massacres: "The Dashnaks . . . denied that the Armenians were conspiring against the Moslems in league with any third group. As late as March 23, just a week before the 'March Days,' the central committee of the Dashnaktsutiun threatened to take the disciplining of such rumormongers into his own hands. The proclamation was indicative of the tense atmosphere in which the population of Baku lied, cut off as it was by Moslems from Tiflis and the north the Caucasus. Unexplained shootings occurred daily; and a duel between the Moslem forces, still weak and underequipped, and the well-armed soviet and Dashnak forces was expected to break out at any moment . . . The Armenians knew that their national hero, General Andranik had evacuated Erzurum on March 11 [1918]"[134] and was preparing to attack Karabakh.

Suny's account of the bombing of the Muslim quarters is different from other versions: "At ten in the morning on April 1 the Committee of Revolutionary Defense sitting in the Hotel

---

[133] R. G. Suny, *The Baku Commune 1917-1918: Class and Nationality in the Russian Revolution* (Princeton, 1972).

[134] Ibid., p. 214.

ANAR ISGENDERLI

Astoria on Morskaia Street, decided that the situation called for the use artillery against the Moslem quarter. A leaflet was issued: In view of fact that the counterrevolutionary party Musavat declared war on the Soviet of Workers', Soldiers' and Sailors' Deputies in the city of Baku and thus threatened the existence of the government of the revolutionary democracy, Baku is declared to be in a state of siege. Bombing of the Azerbaijanis' quarter was begun immediately. The Moslems had not expected the heavy guns to be used and with them against them the rebels could not hold out for long."[135]

Narimanov gives the following account: "At eleven in the morning the influential Moslem Ismayil bey Safataliyev telephoned Dr. Narimanov and pleaded with him to find a way to stop the fighting, which threatened to destroy the Moslem quarter and kill innocent bystanders. An hour later out of the Moslem fortress in the center of the old city came Agu-Dzhafat [or Aga-Javad] with a similar plea. N. Narimanov telephoned Dzhaparidze and relayed the pleas of the Moslems. Dzhaparidze was unwilling to stop the shelling of the Moslem quarter until a delegation from the rebels appeared before the Committee of Revolutionary Defense."[136]

Touching upon the question of the ultimatum by the Committee of Revolutionary Defense delivered to the Muslim delegation, Suny wrote that the head of the Baku Soviet was loath to stop the massacre. In the afternoon on April 1, the Muslim

---

[135] Ibid., p. 221.

[136] Ibid., p. 221, lib. cit.: *Nariman Narimanov, Stat'i i pis'ma s kratkim biografcheskim ocherkom* [Nariman Narimanov: Articles, letters, and short biography] (Moscow, 1925), pp. 5-6.

delegation led by A. Topchubashov arrived at the Astoria. The committee presented them with an ultimatum and demanded that representatives from all Muslim organizations sign the document before the shelling stopped. After some discussion, the Muslims decided to capitulate to the committee's demands. At about four o'clock, the protocol was signed and artillery bombardment halted. Individual shooting continued, however, during the negotiations.[137]

Suny also described the events at the time of issuing of the ultimatum: "Before the ultimatum was signed the Soviet forces advanced slowly, aided by artillery-fire, along Armenian Street, taking Vorontsov Street and the Metropole Hotel. By midday the Moslem headquarters in the Ismailie Building on Nikolaevskaia Street were captured, and Soviet trenches had been advanced as far as Bazzar Street . . . The Armenian soldiers became more brutal as resistance subsided. For a day and a half they looted, killed, and burned in the Moslem quarter. They were indiscriminate in their vengeance, killing even Moslems who were pro-Bolshevik."[138]

That period of the history of Azerbaijan was studied by a well-known Western scholar Audrey L. Altstadt. Her book, *The Azerbaijan Turks: Power and Identity under Russian Rule*, published in 1992, gets to the roots of the problem. Altstadt, unlike most of other foreign authors, traveled to Azerbaijan both in the Soviet times and when Azerbaijan became independent; she was an eyewitness of many events and processes from the ground.

---

[137] Ibid., p. 221.
[138] Suny, op. cit, pp. 223-224.

Altstadt also mentioned that besides disarming Russian soldiers in Ganja, Azerbaijani Turks also disarmed Russian troops in January 1918 at Shamkir station less than forty kilometers west of Ganja.[139] According to Naghi Keykurun Sheykhzamanli, former minister of National Security of Azerbaijani Democratic Republic, the Russian soldiers attacked as one contingent, coming forward ostensibly to surrender their weapons: "Our people's forces seeing Russian treachery counterattacked; fighting continued until nightfall . . . the Russians started throwing their weapons and surrendering. The next day, those Russians were put on trains and sent back to Russia. The weapons were distributed to those who had none. We were not jubilant because of causalities."[140] Altstadt writes, "Numerous Russian causalities and mutual distrust between the two communities contributed to the final rupture of already strained relations between Musavatists and Bolsheviks. It would be the Baku Azerbaijanis who would pay the price in the 'March days.'[141] In January 1918 all political forces but the Musavat desired to gather around the Soviet. The Dashnaks, the Cadets, the Socialist-Revolutionaries and the Mensheviks, who opposed the Musavat's independence claims, supported the idea that 'the Bolshevik government is better than the Musavat.'" For this reason the Azerbaijani National Council was

---

[139] Audrey L. Altstadt, *The Azerbaijan Turks: Power and Identity under Russian Rule*, p. 85.

[140] N. Keykurun, *Azerbaycan istiklalı mücadelesi hatiralari* [Memoirs of the struggle for independence in Azerbaijan] (Istanbul, 1964), pp. 21-22.

[141] Audrey L. Altstadt, op. cit., p. 85.

losing power to the Soviet. Altstadt supported the conclusions of Suny and Swietochowski on the armed conflict: "The 6,000 men of the Baku Soviet faced an estimated 10,000 Azerbaijani troops. The Dashnaks, with 4,000 well-armed and experienced troops, joined to the Soviet force. The next day, on 19 March/1 April, Bolsheviks decided to use artillery against Azerbaijani residential quarters. Shelling forced immediate capitulation and the acceptance of Soviet's ultimatum."[142] After the Azerbaijani representatives accepted the terms, the Dashnaks took to looting, burning, and killing in the Muslim sections of the city. Thousands of Azerbaijani Turks fled the city.[143] Those who could not leave were doomed to be slaughtered. The British vice-consul in Baku, Major Ranald MacDonell, wrote, "Not a single Musulman of any importance remain[ed]."[144] "The exodus shifted the demographic picture even further in favor of nonnative elements. The Baku branch of the National Council was disbanded. The Azerbaijanis, from those 'March Days' until the following August, would play no political role in Baku. There was no obstacle to soviet control over Baku. On the 9 April, all 'bourgeois' newspapers were shut down. Armenians had charge of trade, finance and food supplies."[145]

Altstadt also did not consider the March massacres as the closing point of the events in the South Caucasus. She arrived

---

[142] Ibid., p. 87.

[143] Ibid., p. 89.

[144] MacDonell's report to the War Office (December 5, 1918) cited in *The British Archive Records on the Azerbaijani Democratic Republic* (Baku 2008), pp. 67-75.

[145] Audrey L. Altstadt, op. cit., p. 86.

at a conclusion that the Baku Soviet of People's Commissars was extraneous to the Azerbaijani people. The author accepted the formation of the Azerbaijani Democratic Republic in 1918 as a great political event.

Richard Pipes also wrote on the 1918 massacre and drew inference that the Bolsheviks intentionally accumulated the soldiers who were returning from the Turkish and Persian fronts in Baku to commit unseen crimes.[146] The circumstances are also described in *The History of Azerbaijan's Independence Struggle* by Huseyn Baykara: "Many groups of the armed Russian and Armenian soldiers returning from Turkish and Persian frontlines were billeted in Baku. First Shaumian used pro-Bolshevik Russian soldiers, and then he drew in Armenian soldiers due to their hatred of the Turks and Muslims."[147]

The UK National Archives hold enough records on the 1918 genocide of the Muslim Turks by the Armenian-Bolshevik forces. Some striking examples are provided below.

It is a fact that many rich and influential Armenians who lived outside of the southern Caucasus rendered support to the massacres against the Muslim population. In one case, a group of wealthy Armenians appealed to Charles Marling, the British ambassador to Tehran, to render financial aid to Andranik, the author of ferocities against the Muslim Turks in Nakhchivan, Erivan, Zangezur, Karabakh, and in other provinces of

---

[146] Richard Pipes, *The Formation of the Soviet Union: Communism and Nationalism 1917-1923* (Cambr.,1964), p. 201.

[147] Hüseyin Baykara, *Azerbaycan istiklal mücadelesi tarihi* [History of the struggle for independence of Azerbaijan] (Istanbul, 1975; reprinted: Baku, 1992), p. 256.

Azerbaijan. Notwithstanding the numerous requests and telegrams by the Armenians, the British headquarters refused to aid Armenians directly but offered one million rubles through the Russians.[148]

The news of the British financial assistance to the Armenians caused a great discontent among the Muslims in Ganja and Baku. When the information about the next allocation in the amount of two million rubles to the Armenians reached the members of the Ganja branch of the Azerbaijani National Committee, they arranged inspection of all trains from Baku to Tbilisi to prevent the transfer of money. In many cases, Fatali Khan Khoyski personally supervised such searches. Upon receiving British aid, the Armenian regiment attacked several Kurdish villages and slaughtered their population. After this incident, Lieutenant Colonel Pike, the head of the British mission in Tbilisi, put a veto on financial aid to the Armenian detachments.[149] During the 1918 March massacres of the Muslim Turks, R. MacDonell, the former British vice-consul in Tehran, was in Baku and witnessed the Armenian-Bolshevik unification. According to MacDonell, the massacre "poured oil on the flames" of hatred among the Caucasian Muslims toward the British. MacDonell, a witness of the carnage, voiced his

---

[148] The report of the former British vice-consul to Tehran, then the British official in Tbilisi and Baku—Ranald MacDonell on the events within and outside of Azerbaijan prior to the arrival of the British troops led by General Dunsterville in Baku, September, 1917-August, 1918. See *Azərbaycan Xalq Cümhuriyyəti. Böyük Britaniyanın arxiv sənədləri* [The British archive records on the Azerbaijani Democratic Republic] (Baku, 2008), p. 19.

[149] Ibid., p. 20.

protest before the Armenian National Council and declared that by uniting with the Bolsheviks (in fact, the majority of the Bolsheviks were Armenians) against the Muslims, they had made the biggest mistake in their history, and the entire responsibility for the consequences should be born by the Dashnaktsutiun.[150]

On July 20, 1918, the commander in chief of the British military in India confidentially reported to London that the Armenians had undermined their work among Tatars (meaning the Azerbaijani population). In the report, he noted that the Tatars had become assured that the British had been pursuing a deliberate anti-Muslim policy due to mass killing of Tatars by Armenians.[151]

The geography of the slaughters committed by the Armenian military against the Muslim Turks was not limited to the territories of Turkey and Azerbaijan. The classified telegram sent on December 22, 1918, by Percy Cox, the British acting minister in Tehran, to London confirms that the Council of the Muslim Republics of the Caucasus, which functioned in Tabriz, pleaded with the Spanish consul to inform the governments of the Great Britain and the United States of the Armenian-led massacres of the Caucasian Muslims.[152]

An envoy of the British Foreign Office, who had been an eyewitness of the massacres of the Azerbaijani Turks in Baku, wrote in his "Memo on Situation in Baku" (dated June 11, 1918) that the Armenians joined with the better-armed

---

[150] Ibid.
[151] Ibid., pp. 20-21.
[152] Ibid.

Bolshevik troops and utilized them in the fight against Tatars (Azerbaijanis). Baku became an arena of heavy battles. The crews on the gunboats joined the Bolsheviks and fired on the Muslim quarters of Baku. The Bolsheviks and the Armenians eventually prevailed.[153] In a report on the visit to Azerbaijan, the British ambassador Oliver Wardrop wrote that Azerbaijanis informed him that the local Armenians, supported by the Bolsheviks, had murdered many Muslims. The ambassador concluded that Shaumian was a pseudo-Bolshevik.[154]

George Milne, the commander in chief of the British armies in Salonica, reported to the chief of General Staff on April 6, 1919, "Before occupation of Baku [British troops entered Baku on November 17, 1918] two Turkish regiments defended Shusha from attacks of Andranik's army. Now the Armenians have captured the city and killed the Turks. The government does its best to ensure law and order. One battalion of British soldiers is required to enforce law. The Baku Armenians create a particularly unpleasant situation. The impoverished Armenians joined the Bolsheviks and the underground Dashnaktsutiun. They have no other goal than to take revenge on the Tatars [Azerbaijanis]."[155]

On October 21, 1918, the Persian Ministry of Foreign Affairs appealed to the British diplomatic in connection with the massacres of the Muslim-Turkic population by the Armenians.

---

[153] Ibid.

[154] *Azərbaycan Xalq Cümhuriyyəti. Böyük Britaniyanın arxiv sənədləri* [The People's Republic of Azerbaijan. Archive records of Great Britain] (Baku 2008), p. 24.

[155] Ibid., pp. 21-22.

The appeal read, "The Armenians slaughtered and plundered the Muslims of Erivan, Nakhchivan, Kars and other provinces. Irrespective of their intentions, the Armenians committed all kinds of crimes against Muslims. The Muslim families were dispersed, innocent men and children were murdered, women were humiliated, their belongings were taken away and the villages were destroyed."[156] The Persian Foreign Ministry also requested the British government to give instructions to restrain the Armenians, to prevent crimes and violence, and to protect the civilians.

Oliver Wardrop, the British commander in chief in the Caucasus, also writes on the Armenian ferocities in his report (1919): "The Armenians have recently destroyed 60 Muslim villages in Yeni Beyazit, Alexandropol, and Erivan."[157]

3.2. The Shamakhi Massacres

The old Azerbaijan town of Shamakhi also underwent terrible lootings and other atrocities. The Armenian savageries in the town of Shamakhi and the homonymic *uyezd* are described on 925 sheets of investigational materials arranged in seven volumes.

A. Khasmammedov, the chairman of the Extraordinary Investigation Committee, wrote in a report to the Minister of Justice that the town consisted of two parts—upper, or the Armenian part, and lower, or the Muslim part. The uptown was predominantly populated by Armenians, Molokans

---

[156] Ibid., p. 22.
[157] Ibid., p. 23.

(Russian sectarians), and partially by Muslims while the lower quarters were exclusively populated by Muslims. The Muslim population dominated in the Shamakhi *uyezd*. Armenians and Molokans lived only in six villages. In the past, Muslims lived in concord with Armenians and Molokans, had never afflicted them, and always tried to keep friendly neighboring relations. During the widespread hostilities between Armenians and Muslims in many cities and villages of the South Caucasus in 1905, Shamakhi was one of the rare places where no such incidents occurred.

On March 18, 1918 (Julian calendar), the Armenians mobbed into the Muslim quarter shouting "We have waited for this day for 12 years. This is not 1905, when [czar] Nikolai helped you. Now there is no one to help you. Call your Saint Hezret Abbas to save yourselves."[158] When a Russian doctor, Sazanov, who lived in Shamakhi, accused the Armenians of ruthless crimes against the Muslims on the night of March 19, 1918, the Armenians replied, "We have no compassion for the Muslims, all of them must be annihilated."[159]

The Armenian hostilities against the Azerbaijanis in Shamakhi had begun yet before World War I. The Armenians demonstrated arrogance toward Azerbaijanis and openly insulted their national and religious dignity.

After the February Revolution of 1917, the Armenians became more brusque. After the abolishment of the czarist authorities in Shamakhi, the Armenians covertly captured

---

158   SARA, col.1061, list 1, file 108, sheets 8-10.
159   Ibid., sheet 13.

the armory without informing the *uyezd* Commissar or the Muslim National Council. The Armenians brought weapons and ammunition from various sources to their villages and distributed among the population. The arms were mainly brought by the Armenian soldiers returning from the war. Some of them carried up to three rifles. This activity put the Azerbaijanis on alert. The Azerbaijanis, both in the town and the villages, saw the Armenians taking up arms quickly.

Armenian soldiers from other *uyezds* of the South Caucasus began to accumulate in Medrese village located five miles away from the town. In early March, word leaked out that Armenian detachments of approximately three thousand soldiers armed with rifles and machine guns arrived in Shamakhi from Baku. A delegation from Shamakhi, which included both Muslims and Armenians, was sent to meet the units. The meeting took place in a Molokan village of Gozlu-Chay (Khilimli). The units were asked to give up their arms to the Shamakhi garrison. However, the Armenian commanders refused to yield and declared that their intention was to clean the *uyezd* from robbers, put an end to anarchy, and reinstate normal conditions. They also promised to bypass the town of Shamakhi and head for the Medrese village. On March 15, when the troops were passing by the town, they opened fire at the Muslims. Soon skirmishes pervaded the entire town, resulting in a number of dead and injured from both sides. Toward evening, the shooting gradually ceased. That day, the local Armenian bishop gathered his priests from all Armenian villages of Shamakhi to take a collective oath to live in peace and keep the law. When villagers from Kurdemir proposed to the Armenian leaders to live in concord and awakened to the oath taken by the Armenian priests, the Armenians responded, "The

Muslim clergy may heal the breach with the Armenian priests, but the Armenian people want to fight with Muslims and the British will support them in this cause."[160]

In the morning of March 18, 1918, the Azerbaijani population of Shamakhi woke up to the sound of shooting: the Armenians had surrounded the southern part of the town. The Muslim quarters were fired by cannons and machine guns from the south and rifles from the uptown Armenian quarters in the north. The attack was quite unexpected for the Muslims, who trusted in the vow taken by the Armenian bishop Bagrat on the cross and the Bible that the Armenians would always live in peace and friendship with the Azerbaijanis and would never take up arms against them. The Azerbaijanis, unprepared for the assault, attempted to defend themselves, but they eventually were forced to yield under the pressure of cannonade and machine gun fire. In a few hours, the Armenians intruded into the Muslim-populated Piran-Shirvan quarter on the boundary between the Azerbaijani and the Armenian parts of the town. They began to loot and burn houses and slaughter innocent people. The best-furnished houses of the town, which belonged to the wealthy and well-known Muslims, were put on fire. The mansions of the *uyezd*'s mufti, the Shikhaliyevs, the Hasanovs, the Jabrailovs, Huseynbeyov, Alimirzayev, Efendiyev, the Babayevs, the Maharramovs, the Veysovs, Boyuk bey Huseynov, Haji Vahab Alekberov, and others were among the destroyed property.[161]

The Armenians shot without distinction at men, women, and children running out of burning houses. The Armenians

---

[160] SARA, col.1061, list 1, file 110, sheet 10.
[161] SARA, col.1061, list 1, file 90, sheet 9.

broke into the houses, plundered, killed, and then burned the dwellers. In the evening, the Muslims sent a delegation to the Armenians to solicit a truce. The mission failed and the Armenians did not stop the violence. Fire spread through all quarters, and the next morning, the town was in ruins. There were heaps of corpses in the streets. The Armenians had murdered the Azerbaijanis with unheard and unthinkable cruelty. Remains of women who had been tortured and killed were all over. Their breasts had been cut, abdomens had been torn—they had undergone the cruelest tortures. Children had been nailed alive on the ground. The Armenian ferocities in Shamakhi continued for several days.[162] When the Armenians heard of the approaching Azerbaijani units from Ganja, they retreated to Gozlu-Chay. However, the Armenian forces still outnumbered the Azerbaijani troops. For this reason, the Azerbaijani units were forced to leave Shamakhi after four days. The Azerbaijani soldiers helped the majority of the Muslim population leave the town. In a hurry, people were not able to take even the most necessary things. At the same time, many residents—especially the poor, the sick, the elderly, and the children—were unable to leave the town. On the third day after the withdrawal of the Azerbaijani troops, the Armenian gangs again invaded the town. The atrocities repeated with a yet greater cruelty; the Armenians were merciless in punishing the remaining people. All of the Azerbaijani quarters were reduced to ashes. All mosques of the town, including twelve neighborhood mosques and the eight hundred-year-old

---

[162] SARA, col.1061, list 1, file 40, sheet 8.

Juma mosque, which was the most significant piece of local architecture, were burned along with other sacred places. All Azerbaijani quarters of the town were razed to the ground. No house remained unharmed.[163]

The Azerbaijani nation lost some of its most respected public figures, well-known not only in Shamakhi but in the entire country, during the first and second Armenian attacks on the town. The Armenians killed the *akhund* of the town Haji Jafargulu with particular cruelty. They first pulled his beard, fractured his teeth, gouged his eyes, and cut the ears and the nose. Judge Teymur Bey Khudaverdov, a member of the first Russian State Duma from Shamakhi, Muhammad Aliyev, Hajibaba Abbasov, Ashraf Hajiyev, Haji Abdul Khalil Ahmedov, Haji Abdul Huseyn Zeynalov with his three brothers, Haji Israfil Mammadov, Mir Ibrahim Seyidov, Haji Ibrahim Salamov, Agha Ahmed Ahmedov, Haji Abdul Gasim Gasimov, Eyyub-Agha Veysov, Zeynab Khanum Veysova, Ali-Abbas Bey Ibrahimbeyov, Alakbar Gadirbeyov, Abdur-Rahim Agha Aghalarov, Mehiyyeddin Efendizade, Zakariyye Efendi Mehdi Khalil Oghlu, Ziyeddin Abdullayev, Haji Molla Hasan Zeynalov and his wife, Mahmud Haji-Agha Oghlu, his wife and son, and other respected people of the town were brutally killed.[164]

The Armenians also killed or burned alive many women and children who had taken refuge at Haji Jafargulu's house and courtyard. The members of the Extraordinary Investigation Commission found a lot of human bones at the crime scene. In summer 1918, after pushing Armenians out of Shamakhi,

---

[163] SARA, col.1061, list 1, file 49, sheet 9.
[164] SARA, col.1061, list 1, file 113, sheet 13.

Turks gathered and buried the bodies of the victims of the massacre. The report prepared in October-November 1918 showed that a number of bodies continued to remain unburied in the mosque's yard. In addition, many bones were found in other burned mosques and houses.[165]

The records of the commission described the ruins of several mosques and a number of houses and shops; they also included forty-five photos of mortal remains. According to another record, one of the Armenian leaders, in a conversation with his pals, boasted that during the Shamakhi massacre, he raped and then shot ten Muslim girls with his personal handgun.[166]

A scrutiny confirms that both Armenian attacks on Shamakhi were based on detailed plans elaborated by Dashnaks. The raids were led by Stepan Lalayev, Gavril Karaoglanov, Arshak Gulgangian, Mikael Arzumanov, Karapet Karamanov, Sedrak Vlasov, Samvel Doliev, the Petrosiants, the Ivanovs (father and son), barber Avanesov, Agamalov from Shusha, and others. These names were verified during interrogations of hundreds of witnesses and victims who managed to survive and testified to the Armenian leaders' direct involvement in killings and lootings. The victims testified that the former assistant chief of the *uyezd*, Gavril Karaoglanov, the patron of the Shamakhi Armenian church, Mikael Arzumanov, a well-known merchant, E. Ivanyants, and barber Samvel Doliev, were the initiators and executors of these massacres. The Armenians robbed the possessions of the Azerbaijanis in the amount of over one billion manats in the town of Shamakhi alone.

---

[165] SAPPPMRA, col.277, list 2, file 16, sheet 18.

[166] Ibid., sheet 18.

A. Novatsky, the member of Extraordinary Investigation Commission, prepared a report based on numerous material evidences and witness testimonies, where he proposed to open a criminal case against those who committed crimes, murdered, and plundered the Azerbaijani civilians.[167] The Extraordinary Investigation Commission followed the proposal and decided to open criminal cases against the chief organizers of the massacres and launch a criminal investigation.[168] Besides the town, eighty-six surrounding Muslim villages were also subject to treacherous and surprise attacks by the Armenians.

At dawn of March 18, along with the main offensive on Shamakhi, the Armenian gangs unexpectedly attacked the village of Engekharan located three miles away form the town. The investigation material on the Armenian atrocities in the defenseless village includes a list of 237 villagers torturously killed by the Armenians; the list was compiled based on the witnesses' testimonies.[169] The Armenian attackers beset the village, killed and looted the population, burned the houses, and took captives. The captured children were taken to the Azerbaijani village of Melem and kept there. The Armenians took eighty-eight men to the Molokan village of Chukhuryurd. Short of the village, they entered a garden and shot twelve captives. The rest were taken to the Armenian headquarters in the Medrese village. On the way to Medrese, they killed two more villagers. Only seventy-four Azerbaijanis reached Medrese alive. Soon after the arrival of the Azerbaijani troops

---

[167] SARA, col.1061, list 1, file 108, sheet 10.
[168] Ibid., sheet 5.
[169] SARA, col.1061, list 3, file 40, sheets 3-4.

ANAR ISGENDERLI

from Ganja, relatives of the captives from Engekharan went to Medrese to find out about the prisoners. Near the village, they saw that all captives had been killed and their corpses had been defaced. Ears, noses, arms, and legs were torn apart. There were scorches on chests of many bodies. This fact proves that the Armenians had made fire on the victims' chests when they had still been alive. Besides those who were murdered directly, many Engekharan villagers who managed to run from the massacre died of starvation, cold, and diseases. As per the commission's report, the population of Engekharan halved within those few days.[170]

A report submitted to the Extraordinary Investigation Commission on April 3, 1919, by the police chief of the Shamakhi *uyezd* included a list of villages ruined by the Armenians in the three police districts: nineteen villages in the Gebristan district, forty-one villages in the Medrese district, and twenty-six villages in the Kashun district (eighty-six villages in total).[171] The final report drafted for fifty-three villages included the death toll (including men, women, and children) and the total damage inflicted on each village of the Shamakhi *uyezd*. The report was based on comprehensive investigations (witnesses' testimonies, interrogation protocols of victims, official data on the number of population and the value of their properties, lists of dead and injured, etc.) carried out for each village by the Extraordinary Investigation Commission. The body count and the amount of damage in some of these villages are given below.

---

[170]   SARA, col. 1061, list 1, file 90, sheet 9.
[171]   SARA, col. 1061, list 1, file 85, sheets1-3.

Table 1. Losses in selected villages of the Shamakhi *uyezd* as the result of Armenian massacres in March 1918 [172]

Villages		Death toll among Azerbaijanis				Material damage, in million manats
		Total	Men	Women	Children	
1	Nevahi	925	555	260	140	60
2	Yehyaly	922	360	412	150	22
3	Gubaly Baloghlan	533	250	150	135	90
4	Kalva	500	250	150	100	24
5	Aghsu	500	200	300	-	36.5
6	Tirjan	360	300	40	20	-
7	Baghirly	370	80	150	140	12.5

The investigational reports drafted for other villages reflect a similar aftermath of the massacres. All reports were signed and sealed by the members of the Extraordinary Investigation Commission. Pursuant to the investigation materials, the Armenians killed 8,027 people in fifty-three villages of Shamakhi, including 4,190 men, 2,560 women, and 1,277 children; the gross total amount of damages in these villages was 339.5 million manats in then-year values.[173] The Armenian atrocities against the Azerbaijanis, their property, cattle, and croplands were an actual case of genocide.

3.3. The Guba Massacres

In accordance with a prefabricated plan, the Dashnak-Bolshevik forces were to enter the Guba *uyezd* after

---

[172] SARA, col. 1061, list 4, file 41, sheet 10.
[173] SARA, col. 1061, list 2, file 85, sheet 14.

ANAR ISGENDERLI

occupation of Shamakhi. The Armenians of Khachmaz were informed of this and received additional arms and ammunition. Calling the massacres of the Muslim population of Guba since the beginning of 1918 a tragedy does not fully express the essence of the events. The torturous killings of thousands of civilians—including women, children, and elderly—were a catastrophe. The tragedy in Guba had a pure political motive. Bolshevik soldiers took part in the massacres side by side with the Armenian Dashnak troops. The Armenian tormentors seized the occasion and skillfully exploited the anarchy in the country to launch a vast massacre in Guba.

The tragedy in Guba was featured by extensive advance preparations by the Dashnaks. An interethnic conflict was planned to serve as a pretext for much wider massacre. Members of the Dashnaktsutiun sent telegrams abroad, claiming that the Armenians were oppressed by the Muslims in Azerbaijan. The cables sent by the Guba residents M. Kasparov, H. Hayrapetov, A. Mukanian, and A. Bogdanov assured that the Muslims feuded with the local Armenians, had launched ethnic massacres, destroyed the Armenian and Russian villages, and burned the churches.

Guba was subject to the Armenian violence for three times. The major assault against the province was led by David Gelovani with two thousand soldiers and Sturua, who claimed to be a Bolshevik, with one thousand troops. The assault was preceded by an attack of some two thousand Armenian soldiers led by Muradian. These troops were comprised of the soldiers of the Dashnaktsutiun, which had posed as the closest ally of the Russian Czarism during World War I. These troops were backed by the local Armenian gangs in the number of three hundred gunmen led by Avakov and Vartan.

In the beginning, apart from some one hundred soldiers in Gelovani's disposal in Guba, he received additional reinforcement from Khachmaz. Gelovani writes, "A group of 150 soldiers exclusively comprised of Armenians and led by Lieutenant Aghajanian, and 2 cannons from Khachmaz came to our relief."[174] Appearance of Gelovani and his troops in Guba, his request for reinforcement, and the arrival of a solely Armenian unit points to the fact that the ethnic hostility against the Muslims in the northern provinces of Azerbaijan had been arranged in advance. Thus, in early March 1918, the wealthy Armenian families sold their property and hastily left Guba. When they were inquired about the reason, they replied, "Something is expected between Muslims and us, that's why the Committee has called us back."[175]

Upon arrival in Guba, Gelovani released up to two hundred Armenian military prisoners from jail. As it proceeds from the papers of the Extraordinary Investigation Commission and witnesses' testimonies, the prisoners were the Armenian soldiers who had initiated violence in the region earlier that year. A reputed religious figure educated in the Ottoman Empire, Mohub-Ali Effendi, who resided in the Kuzun village of Gusar together with Hatam Serkarov, a resident of Jaghar village, invoked the local population to rise against the Dashnaks, and with a support from Lezgins of South Dagestan, they rebuffed the aggressors. Muradian managed to escape together with some one hundred soldiers, but up to two hundred Dashnaks

---

[174] SARA, col.879, list 10, file 54, sheet 30.
[175] SARA, col.879, list 13, file 40, sheet 21.

ANAR ISGENDERLI

were taken captives and imprisoned in a jail in the Guba prison at the direction of Mohub-Ali Effendi.[176]

While being banished from Guba, Gelovani blustered to return with trained Armenian punitive detachments. Indeed, ten days after his threats, the Armenian troops armed with cannons and machine guns were dispatched from Baku to Guba.

A gang led by Amazasp began to burn the town all the way from the town gates to the distant hillside quarters. The Dashnaks shot everyone on their way—making no distinction of age or sex—stabbed the wounded with bayonets, and poked out the victims' eyes. Those who missed a chance to run and hide in the nearby forest made unsuccessful attempts to hide in their houses. They were forced out of their houses; some of them were killed right away and the rest taken to the square. Hundreds of people were murdered within several hours.

A number of documents and witnesses' testimonies fortify the fact that the Dashnak leaders skillfully utilized Bolshevik soldiers. One of the witnesses writes, "The Dashnaks went out of control and we had to fight with them on an unequal footing. During a day-long battle we lost 200 men and had to retreat to the Digah village with only 40 men. Amazasp was maddened, but he also became more careful. He gathered all inhabitants of the town in the square and declared that he was the Erzurum Armenian who had decapitated thousands of Turks, burned and destroyed more than 200 Turkish villages: 'I fought against Turks for a long time, and defended the interests of the Armenian people. This is the reason I came here. If you

---

[176]   SARA, col.970, list 8, file 43, sheets 13-14.

make a stand, I will kill all of you to the last man.'"[177] The massacres arranged by the Dashnak-Bolshevik gangs in Guba proved to be fiercer than in other provinces. Another witness testifies, "Amazasp called Harun Hayrapetov, an Armenian from Guba who acted as a guide for the Dashnaks, and told him something. Harun took a piece of paper out of his pocket and began reading. That was a list of 26 rich people of Guba. Amazasp sent some of his armed soldiers for those people. When the soldiers returned only with 6 people, the Dashnak commander threw a fit. 4 of these people were women and the other 2 were teenagers. Amazasp ordered to cut off the heads of the teenagers. The women were made to drink their blood. When they wailed and pounced at the Dashnaks, the soldiers stabbed them with bayonets and chopped them in two with swords. When howling grew in the square, Amazasp aligned the soldiers and ordered to open fire at the unarmed and innocent people. Hundreds of men, women and children were killed. It was hard to realize that a man could be so cruel against a human being. 'I will drink your blood,' said Amazasp and ordered to burn the property of the people from that list. With such behavior he proved that he was the cruelest man and blood-sucker."[178]

Amazasp was tasked by Shaumian to kill all the Muslims in Guba and devastate their towns and villages. Then the massacre should have been explained as a conflict between the Shiites and the Sunnites.

---

[177] SARA, col.879, list 10, file 34, sheets 14-15.
[178] SARA, col.970, list 8, file 113, sheets 6-7.

ANAR ISGENDERLI

According to the investigation papers, the number of the Dashnak-Bolshevik troops that arrived in Guba on May 1, 1918, exceeded five thousand. This made it possible to easily slaughter the unarmed civilians. It is enough to say that almost four thousand people were killed within two days to illustrate the scale of the violence in Guba. This figure equaled to one-fifth of the population of Guba.[179]

Harun Shahbali-Oghlu, an eyewitness of the massacre, remembers the following: "The Armenians killed so many people that the streets of Guba turned into a river of blood. When they prepared to shoot all of the 2,000 captives on the square, a man approached their leader. They said he was a commissar. They talked briefly and the soldiers were again ordered to lower their arms. Women and children were weeping. A husky Armenian with five other men came up to the crowd and began to pick young and attractive women. They took more than fifty women away. When one of their brothers protested, they shot him. His body was thrown on the ground and his eyes were gouged out. An Armenian, with the hands in blood, threw the eyes to the crowd. The people howled. The Dashnaks began to beat the people with buttstocks cussing in the Armenian language. Then they stabbed an old man, who had come forward, with a bayonet. It was a repulsive sight."[180]

Another witness bears out the slaughter: "The Armenians brought mullahs to the central square in Guba. The mullahs were the most respectable elders of the *uyezd*. They had been thrashed. Amazasp called a local Armenian, Harun, well-known

---

[179]   SARA, col.970, list 59, file 20, sheets 14-55.
[180]   SARA, col.970, list 10, file 114, sheet 4.

to everyone. Harun translated the order into the Azerbaijani language: 'Split into two rows, Sunnites and Shiites, and stand face-to-face!' The crowd obeyed. The distance between the rows was about 20-30 yards. Then they brought two rifles and said that they would kill them anyway: 'Those who want to survive have to do what we say. The Sunnites and the Shiites will shoot at each other by turn. We shall leave in peace those who survive.' The first two men were drawn forth and given rifles. One of them was a Lezgin, Muhammed, another was a Shiite elder, Mashadi Mir-Sadig. Neither of them wanted to take the Armenian rifles. The soldiers hit their heads with butts and made them take the rifles. They aimed the rifles at one another. Everyone was stunned. Muhammed, who was comparatively younger, suddenly turned back and killed one of the Dashnaks. In the scuffle Mashadi Mir-Sadig also killed one Armenian. Hundreds of people who attempted to run were killed with machine-guns. The majority of them were women and children. Muhammed was quartered: first they dismembered his arms, and then his legs. His head was cut off and raised up on the tip of a bayonet so that everyone could see it. Mashadi Mir-Sadig's eyes were gouged out, his arms and neck were fractured. That day the Dashnaks destroyed the mosque and killed more than 20 mullahs both from the Sunnites and the Shiites."[181] A. Novatski clarified the details and emphasized that the Dashnaks burned twenty-six mosques merely in Guba, Gusar, and Khachmaz to offend the religious dignity of the Muslims.[182]

---

[181] SARA, col.879, list 10, file 96, sheets 35-36.
[182] Ibid., file 114, sheets 10-11.

The Dashnaks completely demolished a number of Muslim shrines and burned thousands of books on Islam, Oriental history, and literature. The Armenians made a bonfire out of 1,300 books when they burned the *medrese* of Abdur-Rahim Effendi in central Guba. An influential religious leader, Ibrahim Aydemirov, who was an eyewitness of the events, remembers, "There were 6-7 hundred year old books in the Digah Mosque written in the Albanian and the Arabic alphabets. Besides burning the books, the Armenians blew up a rock with Albanian inscriptions on it in a shrine located a mile away from the Mosque."[183]

More than sixteen thousand people were killed in total by Amazasp's gang in Guba during the first five months of 1918. According to different sources and witnesses' testimonies, the death toll included approximately 12,000 Lezgins and over 4,000 Azerbaijani Turks and Muslim Tats. Within few months the allied Dashnak-Bolshevik units devastated 162 villages in Guba; 35 of them were razed to the ground and were never inhabited again.[184]

The Armenian gangs did not confine their crimes solely to Muslims; the Jews of Guba became their victims as well. Investigations revealed that the Armenians killed up to three thousand Jews in Guba during 1918-19. Recent studies have elucidated the names of eighty-one of the Jewish victims.[185]

---

[183] Ibid.
[184] SARA, col.879, list 10, file 45, sheets 10-11.
[185] R. Mustafaev, *Marshy Smerti. Prestuplenia armianstva protiv yevreiskogo naroda* [Marches of death. Armenian crimes against the Jewish nation] (Baku, 2008), p. 26.

According to the records of the Extraordinary Investigation Commission, the majority of casualties among the Jews were children, elderly, and women. Amazasp was at the head of the Jewish blood purge. The bodies of the killed Jews were thrown into the Shimi ravine.[186] Those who managed to escape the slaughters and leave the town fled to Khachmaz and then to Derbent. But not all Jews were fortunate to get away. From hearsay, the list of the Jews killed by Amazasp and his gang was kept in the local synagogue.[187]

The discovery and archeological examinations of mass grave sites in Guba in 2007 confirmed that the people buried there had been tortured prior to being killed. These mass graves proved to be the result of the 1918 genocide against Azerbaijanis and other ethnic groups in Guba.

In the Kurdemir village of the Goychay *uyezd*, Dashnaks burned 56 houses and shops, 127 mansions, and 2 mosques; they also plundered the house of the local *imam*. His precious collection of Quranic commentaries, or tafsirs, was put on fire. Quran itself was desecrated. Jengi (Chayly), Garavelli, Garabujag, Mustafany, Khalil-Gasimbey, Arab-Mehdibeyli, Sadaly, and other villages of the Goychay *uyezd* were completely ruined.[188]

The chairman of the commission, Khasmammadov, wrote to the Minister of Foreign Affairs that there was enough factual material on the Dashnak-Bolshevik atrocities in Baku, Shamakhi, Guba, Goychay, and Javad for the Azerbaijani

---

[186] Ibid., pp.27-28.
[187] Ibid., p. 32.
[188] SARA, col.970, list 10, file 52, sheets 18-19.

delegation to take to the Paris Peace Conference. Besides, the commission possessed documents on the carnage in the Lankaran *uyezd* launched by the armed units of the Armenian colonel Avetisov, the hostilities directed by Colonel Illarinovich in the Javad *uyezd*, and other massacres in the Erivan *guberniya* and in four *uyezds* of the Ganja *guberniya*—Jabrayil, Javanshir, Shusha, and Zangezur.[189]

3.4. The Lankaran Massacres

In mid-March, the Bolshevik units were sent from Baku by sea to disarm the Muslim Savage Division in Lankaran. The operation was spearheaded by the Armenian National Council. The Bolshevik soldiers destroyed and plundered every Muslim village on their way. Astara was destroyed by the Bolshevik gunfire; the majority of people were forced to leave their houses. The villages between Gizilaghaj and Lankaran on the Caspian shore were exposed to bombardment from the steamship *Alexander Jandar*. The massacres were launched in January and peaked in March.[190]

Before the liberation of Baku by the Ottoman army, the Armenian units numbering two thousand soldiers arrived in Lankaran and ruthlessly punished the local population. They insulted Muslims in eateries, refused to pay for meals, and made them dig trenches to defend from the Ottoman army. The Armenian soldiers entered the mosques during the Muslim holy month of Muharram and interrupted the religious rites. On

---

[189]   SARA, col.100, list 2, file 791, sheet 2.
[190]   Ibid., sheet 1.

several occasions, when the Muslims gathered in mosques for religious ceremonies, the Armenians broke into the mosques to burgle the people. The Armenian criminals destroyed hundreds of dwellings and killed thousands of guiltless people in the *uyezd*. From January 1918 until suppression of the so-called Molokan Revolt in August 1919, roughly two thousand people were murdered in the province.[191]

3.5. The Zangezur Massacres

During 1918-20, Zangezur was one of the provinces of Azerbaijan that suffered the most from Armenian ferocities. The Dashnak aggression hampered the links between the *uyezd* and Shusha and partially blocked communication with Jabrayil. The local Muslim population was surrounded by armed gangs in the Armenian villages and well-trained Armenian troops under the command of Andranik. Following the order of the Armenian government, Andranik and his troops marched into Azerbaijani territory and required the Muslims either to yield to Armenian rule or leave Zangezur, claiming that the *uyezd* was part of Armenia's territory. When the Muslim villagers refused to obey, the Armenians initiated wide-scale massacres.

As described in the papers of the Extraordinary Investigation Commission, all Muslim villages in the first police district, most of the villages in the second police district, and a number villages in the third, fourth, and fifth police districts of Sisian province were ruined. Some of the villages were razed to the ground, and the lands under these villages were turned into

---

[191] SARA, col.100, list 2, file 85, sheets 6-7.

plowed field by the Armenians. More than fifty thousand Muslims took refuge in the fourth police district and in the Jabrayil *uyezd*.

A report by the commission stated that 115 Muslim villages in the Zangezur *uyezd* were reduced to the ground by the Armenians; the names of the ruined villages are provided therein. The casualties suffered by Azerbaijanis in Zangezur *uyezd* are laid out in the commission's papers: 3,257 men, 2,276 women, and 2,196 children were murdered, and 1,060 men, 794 women, and 485 children were injured in 115 villages. The total casualties in Zangezur alone summed up to 10,068 people. The report maintained that even these shocking figures do not fully depict the Armenian savagery in the region and suggests that not all Muslim victims were included in the lists since it had been extremely difficult to identify all of them at the time of the wide-scale turmoil.[192]

In the Vagudu village, over four hundred Azerbaijanis rushed into a mosque in search of protection, thinking that the Armenians would not lay hands on a place of worship. But the Armenian vandals surrounded the mosque and threw hand bombs inside, and then they set the mosque on fire and burned people alive. Corpses of children, cut in two, were scattered on the streets of the Sheki village. During the bashing of Irmishli village, the Armenians stabbed infants with bayonets and raised them aloft, and then they quartered their bodies. The Armenians demanded that the Muslim villagers in Agudi convert to Christianity; Agudi's women who refused to change their faith were disgraced.

---

[192]   SARA, col.894, list 4, file 65, sheet 3.

The Armenians sabered nine bedridden Muslims in the Chullu village. In the Baghibeyli village, an Azerbaijani family of seven was taken out of their house and burned alive by the Armenians. Arms, legs, heads were chopped away, and bodies were defaced so badly that it was impossible to identify the dead.[193] These episodes were realized in Zangezur under the direct command of Andranik during summer and fall of 1918.

Over one hundred Muslim villages in Zangezur were shattered. Tens of thousands of cattle and hundreds of thousands of sheep and goats were driven away. Gardens, cornfields, and pastures were burned; the entire economy of the province was wrecked. The population suffered roughly one billion manats of material losses.

In November, the Armenian gangs launched military operations against the Muslim villagers of Okhchu, Atgiz, Shabadan, and Piravdan. From December 1919, Armenians intensified their attacks against the Muslim population of Zangezur.[194]

The atrocities of the Armenian nationalists in Zangezur became more severe in the beginning of 1920. The Armenian Republic was the sole initiator of all incidents in Zangezur since January 1920. The main goal was to ethnically cleanse Zangezur from the Muslims and extend the Armenian jurisdiction over the *uyezd* under the auspices of the Paris Peace Conference. Over ten thousand regular troops of the Ararat Republic were involved in the ethnic cleansing operations hand in hand with the Armenian gangs.

---

[193] SARA, col.894, list 8, file 44, sheet 3.
[194] SARA, col.894, list 4, file 65, sheet 8.

ANAR ISGENDERLI

From January 1920, the reports on the massacres in Zangezur received by the parliament and the government of the Azerbaijani Republic and the party leaders were more and more alarming.

A telegram addressed to the Parliament of Azerbaijan on January 21, 1920, by a member of the Parliament, Jalil Sultanov, read, "It has been four days now since the Armenian gangs along with the regular army have been attacking Zangezur using artillery and machine-guns . . . We suffer great casualties. The people flee in fear in search for protection . . . On behalf of the miserable population of the *uyezd* I plead with you to stop protesting on paper and take active measures. Please save one of the most gorgeous places in Azerbaijan from being totally obliterated. Karabakh will be next to share Zangezur's fate. You will be held liable for loosing these lands before the Azerbaijani people and Azerbaijan."[195]

On January 22, the Jabrayil School supervisor, Huseyn Akhunzade, sent a wire to the Parliament: "Since morning of January 19 the Armenian armed forces have been keeping the Muslim villages along the front from Zangezur and Khojahan to Galadere under artillery and machine gun fire. Six villages are totally ruined, nine villages are in fire. The Armenians have no mercy for women or children and cruelly kill the Muslims and destroy their villages. The Muslims have no protection against the aggressors and can survive only by fleeing and leaving their property behind."[196]

The Azerbaijani population was driven to despair by the carnage initiated by the Armenian nationalists in Zangezur

---

[195] SARA, col.895, list 1, file 299, sheet 20.
[196] Ibid., sheets 31-33.

and the inadequate response by the authorities. On January 23, 1920, Huseyn Akhundzade sent another wire with the following message: "Please accept my sincere condolences for the Zangezur Muslims. No matter how loud the Zangezur population cried, nobody heard them, their wail could not get across the Zangezur mountains, valleys and hamlets. Old women were disgraced, headless bodies of innocent infants stained with their blood are scattered in fields. Young women are taken captive and dishonored by the Armenians. Only few men remain in Zangezur able to stand against the Armenians. But they are also desperate. We appeal to our fellow believers and call them to respond to our pleas for help to stop the killing of our brothers, sisters, and innocent children."[197]

Jalil Sultanov writes in his third telegram sent on January 23 to the Parliament directly from the battlefield: "The Zangezur *uyezd* was evened with the ground by the regular army, which arrived from Erivan with ten cannons and numerous machine-guns. There are roughly 10,000 soldiers in the regular Armenian army. The population, desponded to receive aid from the Government, appeals to all Azerbaijani Turks. According to the information received, tomorrow Armenians will attack the Jabrayil *uyezd* from Zangezur. Their goal is to join with the Karabakh Armenians and subsequently interrupt our communication with Nakhchivan, and thus solve both Karabakh and Nakhchivan issues once and for all. It is high time to stop protesting on paper and expose the real face of the Armenian traitors, who have annihilated over 200,000 Muslims of Zangezur. I beg you to take urgent measures to

---

[197] Ibid., sheets 8-12.

rescue at least the Shusha and the Jabrayil *uyezds*. Every minute counts. Delay in this matter equals to crime and betrayal of the nation and the motherland."[198]

In August 1918, the massacres of the Azerbaijanis in the Igdir and the Echmiedzin *uyezds* were arranged under the command of General Dro (Drastamat Kanayan). By his order, more than sixty Muslim villages were destroyed and burned. The population suffered extreme cruelties.

The units under Andranik attacked Aghbulag, Ardanish, Beriyabad, Emirkheyir, Yanigtepe, Golkend (Kara-Koyunlu), Toghluja, Chaykend, Jivikhly, Jil, Shorcha, and other villages of Chemberekend province and cruelly tortured and killed the people, destroyed the villages, looted the possessions of the Muslims, and slashed with sabers the women, the elderly, and the children who had failed to run away. Though the Azerbaijanis comprised the majority in Echmiedzin in 1918, most of the villages in the province were subject to atrocities by the Armenians. As a fact, the Ayarly village underwent an absolute genocide in 1918. Most of the seven hundred villagers were tortured and killed, and the rest were expelled from their dwellings and were destined to die in the mountains.[199]

The population of another Azerbaijani village, Garghabazary—some eight hundred people—underwent tortures and was murdered by the Armenian military. The village was pillaged, destroyed, and burned. The Gemerli village did not escape disaster as well. Approximately five hundred

---

[198] Ibid., sheets 18, 22, 26.
[199] Ibid., sheet 20.

Azerbaijani villagers were killed by the Armenian military, and the rest had to leave their dwellings. The majority of Azerbaijanis in Yukhary Garkhun, Yukhary Turkmenli, Kichik Zeyve, Kurekenli, Mammadabad, Molla Dursun, Haji Gara, Hajilar, Haramly, and other villages of Echmiedzin was forced to run in order to survive the genocide.[200]

In 2004, the Republican Party of Armenia published the booklet *Garegin Nzhde i ego uchenie* (Garegin Nzhde and his teaching) dedicated to the events that occurred in Erzurum, where the Armenian barbarism is acknowledged as well: "During the 2 years of ceaseless fighting the Syunik government lost only several dozens of fighters, while the enemy had 15,000 dead. About 200 villages of the Turks and the Tatars [Azerbaijanis] were returned to the Armenian peasantry."[201]

3.6. The Erivan Massacres

Up to 200 Azerbaijani villages in the Erivan *uyezd* were laid flat prior to March 1918; 62 Azerbaijani villages in the Echmiedzin *uyezd* were leveled with the ground before September 1919. All villages but a few in the Zengibasar (the Erivan *uyezd*) and the Vedibasar provinces were shattered, and the population was cruelly killed; those who remained alive fled in search of shelter. The fleeing families took refuge in Persia, Turkey, and other provinces of Azerbaijan.[202]

---

[200] Ibid., sheets 31-33.
[201] *Garegin Njde i ego uchenie* [Garegin Nzhde and his teaching] (Yerevan, 2004), p. 8.
[202] SARA, col.895, list 1, file 299, sheets 8-12.

The Vartanly village in the Gugark province lived through a similar tragedy: In mid-April, the Armenian troops assembled the Azerbaijani peasants in a hut under the pretext of holding a meeting. Around 120-150 people were forced into the hut. Priest Vahan opened the meeting and spoke of friendly coexistence of the two communities in the same village. Suddenly, several armed Armenians entered and took the priest out. Then they locked the door and threw a thatch dipped in oil into the hut from the roof. The people—including children, elderly, and women—screamed louder as they were getting stifled from the smoke; many of them fainted, and the rest rushed to punch the door. The unarmed people resisted in vain.[203]

In 1918, the Armenian military forces carried out an ethnic cleansing of Azerbaijanis in the Kotayk district located in northeast of Erivan. Prior to the 1918 massacres, Azerbaijanis constituted majority of the district residents. However, by that time, Azerbaijanis had been torturously expelled from Avdallar, Artiz, Ashaghy Gakht, Bashkend, Bozkosa, Gayakharaba, Garachala, Garachorek, Gizgala, Gurbaghaly, Damagirmez, Dellekli, Ekerek, Zer, Yelgovan, Yellije, Kamal, Kenkhan, Kerpijli, Goykilse, Gulluje, Nurnus, Okhchu Galasy, Tezeharab, Chobangorukmez, and other villages of the district. The majority of the exiled population was killed by Andranik's gangs and troops of the Dashnak government.[204] In April 1920, the *Azerbaijan* newspaper reported, "Not a single Azerbaijani family remains in the Goyche province. At present, 84 Muslim villages rest in ruins in the Yeni Beyazid

---

[203] SARA, col.894, list 1, file 201, sheet 18.
[204] Ibid., sheets 30, 31, 32.

REALITIES OF AZERBAIJAN 1917-1920

uyezd, 22 of them have been destroyed in April. Over 15,000 families from Dashkend, Goshabulag, Sariyagub, Bash Shorcha, Ashagy Shorcha, Soghangulu-aghaly, Aghkilse, Zod, Gulu, Aghaly, Boyuk Garagoyunlu, Kichik Garagoyunlu, Zerzibil, Edli, Inekdagh, Garaiman, Kesemen, Bashkend, Bala Merze, Shishgaya, Bash Haji, Geribgaya villages have fled for safety and left their possessions behind. Now Armenians have taken over their property valued at hundreds of millions or even billions [of manat]."[205] Most of the population of West Azerbaijan—the present territory of the Republic of Armenia with roughly 565,000 people—were cruelly killed or ousted from their homeland as a result of the genocide executed by Andranik's brigandish troops and the Dashnaks in 1918-20.[206]

An Armenian historian, Z. Korkodyan, wrote in his book titled *The Population of Soviet Armenia in 1831-1931* that a little more than ten thousand Turks (Azerbaijanis) remained in the area by 1920 when Soviet rule was established in Armenia.[207] 211 Azerbaijani villages in the Erivan *guberniya* and 92 Azerbaijani villages in the Kars province were looted, ruined, and burned in 1918. One of the numerous appeals of the Azerbaijanis of Erivan mentioned that 88 villages were destroyed, 1,920 households were burned, and 132,000 Azerbaijanis were killed in Erivan—the historically native province for Azerbaijanis—over a period of several months. The violence initiated by the Armenian punitive forces and the policy of "Armenia without the Turks," then pursued by the Dashnak government, led to

---

[205] Ibid., sheet 33.
[206] Ibid., sheet 34.
[207] Ibid., sheet 38.

drastic decrease in the number of the Azerbaijani population in the Erivan *guberniya* from 375,000 in 1916 to 70,000 in 1922.[208]

Hovhannes Katchaznouni, one of the leaders of the Dashnaktsutiun Party, writes, "We were officially at war with Azerbaijan, because we were actually fighting with them in Karabakh. There were often clashes in Gazakh too. Inside the country, at certain places like Aghbaba, Zod, Zengibasar, Vedibasar, Sherur-Nakhchevan, Zangezur etc. many bloody battles were fought with the native Muslim inhabitants."[209]

The leader of the Dashnak government admitted that hostilities of all kinds were launched against the Muslims in the above provinces. Hovhannes Katchaznouni writes, "We were not able to establish order by means of administrative methods, in the Muslim regions; we were obliged to use arms, send troops, demolish and massacre . . . In important points such as Vedibasar and Şarur-Nakhichevan we were not able to establish our authority even with arms; we lost and receded."[210]

The invasion of Baku by the Eleventh Red Army on April 27 and subsequent subjugation of all other parts of Azerbaijan thwarted the accomplishment of the mission of the Azerbaijani government on ensuring territorial integrity of the country. A number of territories, including Zangezur, were annexed to Soviet Armenia. The massacres of the Muslim population in

---

[208] Ibid., sheet 31.
[209] H. Katchaznouni, *The Armenian Revolutionary Federation (Dashnagtzoutiun) Has Nothing to Do Anymore* (New York: Armenian Information Service, 1955).
[210] Ibid.

1918-20 thus proved to be a policy of genocide deliberately planned and executed by the Dashnaktsutiun toward the establishment of *Great Armenia*.

3.7. The Massacres in Maku, Khoy, and Urmia

The people of Maku, Khoy, and Urmia still keep memory of the slaughters carried out there by the Dashnaks in conjunction with the Aisors in 1918, when South Azerbaijan (now in Iran) had already been conquered by the Russian army. During the lurid events remembered as the Urmia Tragedy, Muslims suffered heavy casualties, and the majority of captives were young Muslim women.[211] The Armenians of Urmia plotted to create a state of Free Armenia with the support of the Russian occupation army in South Azerbaijan. Upon withdrawal from South Azerbaijan, the Russian army handed much of their weapons to the Armenian units so that they could effectively pursue their goal. Despite ethnic and religious differences, Muslims had always demonstrated a kind attitude toward Armenians who had been living comfortably in Azerbaijan for centuries. Nevertheless, thousands of Urmians were tortured and murdered for reasons unclear to them.[212]

In March 1918, Russia withdrew from World War I, and its uncontrolled troops began to leave the Caucasus. The Armenians, who had massacred the population of South Azerbaijan, also fled Urmia assisted by the Russians. Approximately ten thousand

---

[211] M. Mammadzade, *Ermənilər və İran* [Armenians and Persia] (Istanbul, 1927; reprinted: Baku, 1993), p. 9.

[212] Ibid., p. 22.

people left the province in a hurry, taking their most valuable belongings with them. That was the eventual outcome of the Armenian aggression in South Azerbaijan.[213]

Aisors, the Assyrian tribes that settled in northwest Iran who had been living side by side with Azeri Turks and enjoyed their benevolence, were engaged in atrocities against Muslims as well. Urmia, Khoy, Tebriz, Selmas, and other provinces of South Azerbaijan witnessed terrible crimes committed by Armenian and Aisor gangs. The Armenians were led by Agha Petros. The Aisors' commander was Marsimon.[214]

Once, Armenian criminals killed 1,500 Azerbaijanis overnight.[215] This fact is described in writings of Sayyed Ahmad Kasravi, Sayyed Jafar Pishavari, and Dr. Salamullah Javid. Kasravi writes, "The Azerbaijani families of Urmia were robbed; the survivors were gathered in a public building. The miserable people had been hungry and thirsty for several days. Many of them were very reputed people. The bazaar was closed and people could not buy anything; after the pillage they had nothing left in their houses."[216] The records of the period testify that an epidemic of cholera spread in Urmia and Selmas, and the majority of the starving people died of cholera.

After the declaration of independence of the Armenian Republic in May 1918, the Dashnak leader, Andranik, with five

---

[213] S. Onullahi, *Ermǝni millǝtçilǝri vǝ İran* [Armenian nationalists and Persia], referring to Sayyed Ahmad Kasravi, *Tarikhi hijdeh sale-ye Azerbaijan* (Baku, 2002), p. 53.
[214] Ibid., p. 54.
[215] Ibid., p. 58.
[216] Ibid., p. 59.

thousand troops, attacked Khoy. At that time, Khoy was one of the liveliest cities of South Azerbaijan. Mosques, bazaars, and streets were full of people who rumored that Armenians had raped the women, roasted the flesh of the Turks in Erzinjan and Trabzon, and made the people eat it.[217] On June 24, 1918, armed Dashnak troops led by Andranik surrounded Khoy. The men took up arms to defend the town. The women and children helped by providing food for the town defenders. Several houses were destroyed due to shellfire by the Dashnaks; an artillery shell hit a house and killed two men.

With the support of the Russian army, the Dashnak troops, under the command of Petros, moved from Urmia and attacked Selmas. There they engaged in a few daylong fierce battle. The Armenian troops, reinforced by the Assurs (or Aisors), won the battle of Selmas and victoriously returned to Urmia. With the Armenian troops deployed in Urmia, killing of the local Muslims was a widespread and ordinary practice. Meanwhile, Andranik launched another offensive on Khoy. Andranik intended to occupy Khoy, establish Minor Armenia in South Azerbaijan, and join with Great Armenia in the future upon realization of the ambitious plans.[218] The Ottoman command in Khoy required the riflemen of the town to join the defense. The two sides engaged in an unequal battle near Evoghlu. The Armenians heavily outmanned and thus defeated the Ottomans. Some of the wealthy population of Khoy had left the town for Tabriz, but the brave and dignified defenders of the town vouched to stand against the enemies till the end.

---

[217] Ibid.
[218] Ibid., pp. 61-62.

At night, the defenders gathered in one of the mosques and formed a military commission charged with the organization of defense. The next day, the Dashnaks lined up three hundred meters off the town. Again, the Armenians brought artillery and plenty of ammunition. Though the town's gunmen had never been to a war, they fought very vehemently. By nightfall, the Armenians had seized a part of the town.[219]

In those tragic days, the Ottoman army rendered support to the Azerbaijani people and rescued them. Involvement of the Ottoman forces in South Azerbaijan prevented the slaughter of thousands of people.

In the meantime, the Ottoman army was moving toward Khoy from Selmas. The people of Khoy, inspired by the approach of the Ottoman troops, made a fierce effort to defend themselves. Ottoman forces arrived to rescue the people of Khoy just when the Dashnaks had entered the town and launched the massacre of the residents. Andranik and his troops had to retreat.[220]

Andranik's troops were defeated by joint efforts and were forced to retreat. The failure to capture Khoy became the turning point in the realization of the Armenian campaign and undermined their plans for Urmia.[221] Defeated in Khoy, the Dashnak and the Aisor units prepared for a decisive attack on Urmia. The Russian command intended to deploy the troops on the Urmian shore by the steamship *Chernozoyev*. The Dashnaks and the Aisors assisted in a sailboat. The well-trained

---

[219] Ibid., p. 62.
[220] Ibid.
[221] Ibid.

unit of 180 gunmen was to land and suddenly invade the city. Upon landing, the gang encountered the resistance of Turks and Azerbaijanis and was defeated, resulting in failure of the Armenian plan to capture Urmia.[222]

---

[222] Ibid.

ANAR ISGENDERLI

CHAPTER 4

PROCLAMATION OF THE AZERBAIJANI DEMOCRATIC REPUBLIC AND ITS ACTIVITIES

4.1. The Azerbaijani Democratic Republic: the Period in Tiflis

O N MAY 28, 1918, the Muslim National Council held its opening sitting chaired by the deputy chairman Hasan Agayev in the palace of the former Russian governor of the Caucasus. Mustafa Mahmudov acted as the secretary of the sitting. After impassioned and comprehensive debates, the Interim National Council adopted the *Declaration of Independence*, which proclaimed the establishment of the independent Azerbaijani Democratic Republic in south and southeast Transcaucasia.[223] The Declaration, or "Misagi-Milli" (the National Vow), which consisted of six clauses, was approved by twenty-four votes (two of the delegates—Sultan Majid Ganizade and Jafar Akhundov—abstained). The *Declaration of Independence* became the first constitutional act in the history of Azerbaijan and affirmed Azerbaijani statehood

---

[223] SARA, col.970, list 1, file 1, sheets 49-50.

in the form of a democratic republic. This legal and political document declared the establishment of the Azerbaijani state, defined the territory under its jurisdiction, and ascertained the governing principles of the state. The Declaration contained all attributes of a democratic statehood—authority vested in the people; representation of civil and political rights of the citizens; establishment of conditions for freedom of all people regardless of nationality, religion, class, ideology, and gender; and finally, separation of powers. By acknowledging these principles as fundamental for functioning of the state, the Declaration reaffirmed the determination of the Azerbaijani people to establish a sovereign and democratic state governed by law. The *Declaration of Independence* marked the transition of the Azerbaijani nation from a *nation-culture* status to an absolutely different legal-political and moral-psychological status of a nation-state. On May 30, radio and telegraphic messages announcing the independence of Azerbaijan were dispatched to the major capital cities of the world.

Following the adoption of the *Declaration of Independence*, the national council designated nonpartisan Fatali Khan Khoyski in charge of the formation of the government. After an hour of adjournment, Khoyski announced the makeup of the first cabinet, which included nine ministers from the Musavat, the Muslim Socialist Coalition, the Hummet, the Ittihad, and the nonpartisans.[224]

On May 29, the Muslim National Council held its second sitting in Tiflis chaired by Hasan Agayev. Prime Minister Khoyski informed the attendees of negotiations between

---

[224] Ibid., sheets 49-50.

the members of the Azerbaijani and the Armenian National Councils on the border delimitation issues. Khoyski told them that the Armenians needed a political center to establish an Armenian federation, and cession of Erivan to Armenians was inevitable since the Turkish army had captured Alexandropol (Gumri). Other speakers—including Khalil Khasmammadov, Mammad Yusif Jafarov, Akber Aga Sheykhulislamov, and Mahammad Maharramov—noted that cession of Erivan is both a historical necessity and inevitable disaster at the same time. Out of twenty-eight delegates present at the meeting, sixteen voted in favor of the proposal, one voted against, and the remaining three abstained from voting. The issue of establishment of a confederation with Armenians was brought up for discussion as well. After brief debates over the proposal of future integration of the Azerbaijani and the Armenian councils into a confederation, the delegates considered the idea acceptable and unanimously voted in its support.[225]

On May 29, Prime Minister Khoyski wrote a letter to Foreign Minister Mammad Hasan Hajinski, who was in Batum negotiating with the Ottomans: "We put an end to all disputes with Armenians, they will accept the ultimatum and stop fighting. We ceded Erivan to them." However, on June 1, during the sitting of the national council, three of its members from Erivan—Mir Hidayat Seyidov, Baghir Rzayev, and Nariman Narimanbeyov—protested against the cession and signed a joint note. The council resolved to append the note to the minutes of the sitting without further discussion.[226]

---

[225] Ibid., sheets 51-52.
[226] Ibid., sheets 53-54.

Based in Tiflis, the national council and the government fully realized that the main director of all events in the South Caucasus was the Ottoman government. Any vital decision linked to the region required approval by the Ottomans. That is why the national council and the government placed their hopes in the negotiations in Batum.

On June 4, delegates from the three newly independent states of the South Caucasus—Azerbaijan, Georgia, and Armenia—finally negotiated and signed separate treaties with the Ottoman state in Batum. The chairman of the national council, Rasulzade, and Foreign Minister Hajinski signed the treaty for Azerbaijan. The Treaty of Batum became the first agreement concluded between the Azerbaijani Democratic Republic and a foreign state. Among the eleven clauses of the treaty, the fourth article had a particular importance for Azerbaijan. The article affirmed the commitment of the Ottoman government to render military assistance to the Republic of Azerbaijan in order to maintain peace and stability and assure the security of the country, if necessary. At the time of conclusion of the Batum Treaty, the national council and the national government still functioned in Tiflis.

Meanwhile, the Dashnak-Bolshevik army of the Baku Soviet of People's Commissars, led by Shaumian, launched an offensive on Ganja. In the teeth of the critical military situation, the Azerbaijani representatives in Batum, Mammad Emin Rasulzade and Mammad Hasan Hajinski, appealed to the Ottoman government with request of rendering military aid to Azerbaijan in conformity with the Article 4 of the treaty. The appeal was approved, and the Ottomans sent the Caucasus Army of Islam to lend support to Azerbaijan in the days of hardships. The Ottoman secretary of war, Enver Pasha, ordered to allocate a loan in the amount of two million Turkish liras as an initial aid to Azerbaijan; additionally, fifty thousand liras were disbursed monthly on supply expenditures of the Turkish army in Azerbaijan. Besides, in the meeting with M. A. Rasulzade in Istanbul, Enver Pasha stressed the importance of building a national army in Azerbaijan.

On June 13, 1918, the Azerbaijani National Council convened its sixth (and last) meeting in Tiflis. The agenda included the alarming news from Erivan about massacre of the Azerbaijani population by Armenians. The council member, Ibrahim Agha Vakilov, who had returned from Erivan, informed the attendees of the miserable conditions of Azerbaijani refugees and proposed to allocate 150,000 manats for delivery of humanitarian aid. As reported by Vakilov, the number of Muslim refugees from the Erivan *guberniya* had reached 150,000; 206 Muslim villages had been destroyed, and villagers had been tortured by Dashnak gangs. In the view of the situation, the council appealed to the Turkish military command to supply food to the Erivan refugees and facilitate the return of the expelled Muslim population to their homes.[227]

4.2. Establishing the Azerbaijani Democratic Republic in Ganja

After finalizing all preparations, the national council and the cabinet of the Azerbaijani Democratic Republic relocated to Ganja on June 16, 1918. Reactionary and narrow-minded

---

[227] SARA, col.970, list 1, file 6, sheet 1.

groups among the bourgeoisie and landlords uninvolved in the national council attempted to bar the council from power through the commander of the Turkish troops in Azerbaijan, Nuri Pasha. These groups were fervid supporters of Azerbaijan's annexation to Turkey and, hence, undertook an active campaign against the national council. The strained relations between the council and the command of the Caucasus Army of Islam, which was also based in Ganja, gradually increased. By interfering in domestic affairs of an independent state, Nuri Pasha disobliged Khoyski's government and provoked a political crisis.

In view of prevailing anarchy in the country and foreign and domestic challenges, on June 17, the national council—after lengthy debates—enacted to establish a new cabinet with Khoyski in the chair and entrust it with ample powers; in the end of the meeting the council decided to dissolve itself.[228]

Khoyski's second cabinet assumed its functions under very complicated conditions in Ganja. The government undertook a number of actions to keep up political and economic life, eliminate anarchy, restore railroads, and establish postal and telegraphic communication among the provinces of Azerbaijan. The primary goal of the government was to overturn the Baku Soviet of People's Commissars, set up by Shaumian shortly after the March genocide of 1918, and turn Baku into the capital city of the country. These were the subjects of intense talks between the government and the Ganja-based Ottoman Caucasus Army of Islam.

---

[228] SARA, col.970, list 1, file 1, sheet 48.

4.3. The Caucasus (Ottoman) Army of Islam and the Rescue Campaign on Azerbaijan

The year 1914 was marked by the instigation of World War I, launched for the redistribution of influence in the world. West's main interest in the war was capturing new lands and gaining new markets. The Ottoman Empire, also engaged in the war, undertook two tactical ploys: according to the plan drafted by Jamal (Cemal) Pasha, the Ottomans attempted to reunite the lost lands of the caliphate under Ottoman rule. In the end of December 1914, the Turkish Army, headed by Enver Pasha, attacked Russian troops on the Caucasian Front. The historical battle of Sarikamish was a disaster for the Ottoman Army. Cold and foul weather and hunger and typhus led to a very high mortality among soldiers wearing thin and off-grade summer uniforms in the middle of winter. The constantly reinforced Russian army smashed the Ottomans at Sarikamish and took ninety thousand Ottoman soldiers and officers as war prisoners. The majority of captive Turkish soldiers were killed just on the spot. The severe winter helped the Russian command in this task. A portion of the war prisoners was brought to Baku by rail and sent to Nargin and Bulla islands in the Caspian. The remaining captives were exiled to Siberia. Thus, the initial stage of both Jamal Pasha's pan-Islamism movement on Sinai Front and Enver Pasha's pan-Turanism campaign in the Caucasus was catastrophic for the Ottomans.[229]

---

[229] A. N. Kurat, *Türkiye ve Rusya* [Turkey and Russia] (Ankara, 1990), p. 266.

The year 1917 was marked by two major events that changed the course of the Great War: the February Revolution and the October coup in Russia. In March 1918, Russia acceded to the Treaty of Brest-Litovsk with the Central powers led by Germany. In accordance with the terms of the treaty, the Russian army was to withdraw from eastern Anatolia; Ardahan, Batum, and Kars were to be surrendered by Russians in a short time. Under these circumstances, the Treaty of Brest-Litovsk gave Enver Pasha a chance to realize his Caucasus plan. During the Great War, Armenian armed forces, extensively supported by the Russian army in the killings of hundreds of thousands of Anatolian Turks, embarked on the plan for establishment of Great Armenia. But the Armenian military units could not accomplish the vicious plans and had to retreat to the South Caucasus. Here, the Armenian detachments caught the opportunity to commit killings of the Muslim population in the southern, western, and northern provinces of Azerbaijan. The situation required involvement of the Ottomans to rescue Azerbaijanis from the Dashnak-Bolshevik violence. Therefore, since the beginning of 1918, the Ottoman government had kept the Caucasus Campaign in its agenda to utilize the historical chance.

After declaring independence in May 1918, the newly established Azerbaijani Democratic Republic announced Ganja as its temporary capital until the liberation of Baku from the Soviet rule. The other new republics, Georgia and Armenia, announced respectively Tiflis and Erivan as their capitals. The founders of the Azerbaijani Democratic Republic now faced the challenge of vitalization and empowerment of the new statehood in the view of the following hindrances:

- The Azerbaijani Republic was declared in a foreign territory, Tiflis.
- The new state had no military capacity to defend its territory.
- Baku was occupied by the Baku Soviet troops, which numbered twenty thousand soldiers.
- The political, economic, and military situation in Azerbaijan hindered resolution of the above issues.
- Russia's Soviet leadership exerted all efforts to keep Azerbaijan under its influence in order to benefit from Baku's oil.
- Great Britain and Germany, enemies during World War I, each had distinct plans for Azerbaijan.

These were the main factors that necessitated the conclusion of a peace treaty between the Azerbaijani Democratic Republic and the Ottoman government in order to ensure the Ottoman military assistance to Azerbaijan in case of any hostile situation in the territory of the latter.

On May 11, 1918, prior to declaration of the Azerbaijani Democratic Republic, leaders of the northern Caucasus nations of the Terek and Dagestan regions declared independence of the North Caucasus Mountaineers Republic. With the goal to ensure the Ottoman interests in the Caucasus, Enver Pasha recognized the North Caucasus Republic and gave instructions on rendering military assistance to the new statehood.

Recognition of the North Caucasus Mountaineers Republic and then the Azerbaijani Democratic Republic by the Ottomans irritated Soviet Russia's leaders, who viewed the spread of the Ottoman influence in Azerbaijan and the North Caucasus as an eventual loss of these territories. They were especially worried to lose access to the Baku oil, which would cause heavy damage to the Russian economy. On that score, on May 30, 1918, the Russian commissar of foreign affairs, Georgy Chicherin, sent a note to the Ottoman government with a protest against recognition of independence of the Caucasian states.[230] But the Ottoman government had no intention to renounce its decision or adjourn the march on Caucasus.

The Russian withdrawal from the war, uncontrolled activities of the Russian army at the front line, and the Armenian-launched massacres in Azerbaijan prompted Azerbaijanis to appeal for help from the Ottomans. To that end, in October 1917, a delegation of the Azerbaijani Turks met with the Ottoman's Sixth Army Command in Mosul. The delegation returned to the Caucasus with three Ottoman officers dispatched to examine the situation on the ground. The officers returned to the headquarters in Mosul and reported of favorable conditions for a military expedition.[231]

---

[230] *Bol'sheviki v bor'be za pobedu sotsialisticheskoy revolutsii v Azerbaijane. Dokumenty i materialy. 1917-1918 gg.* [Bolsheviks in the fight for the victory of the Socialist Revolution in Azerbaijan. Documents and records. 1917-1918.] (Baku, 1957), p. 98.

[231] N. Yucer, *Birinci dünya savaşında Osmanlı ordusunun Azerbaycan ve Dağıstan harekatı* [The campaigns of the Ottoman Army in Azerbaijan and Dagestan during World War I] (Ankara, 1996), p. 55.

ANAR ISGENDERLI

On February 16, 1918, Enver Pasha issued an order to establish an entity to be headquartered in Tehran with the purpose to help the Muslim nations of the Caucasus, Dagestan, Turkestan, and Russia.[232] The order instructed to appoint confident and devoted officers at the head of the campaign: Lieutenant Colonel Nuri Bey (stepbrother of Enver Pasha) was appointed the head of the Tehran Central Staff; Lieutenant Colonel Shevket Bey was assigned to lead troops to Dagestan; Captain Nazim Javad Bey was put in charge of the expedition to Afghanistan; and other officers under command of Halil Pasha were to be sent to other regions of the Caucasus and Turkestan. Enver Pasha also ordered to send a mission headed by Nuri Bey to Azerbaijan to establish branch organizations in the provinces predominantly populated by Azerbaijani Turks and prepare the ground for foundation of the Army of Islam manned by the local Muslims. Lieutenant Colonel Nuri Bey was promoted to honorary general rank to exclude any doubt of his commanding authority. All other officers in the expedition to Azerbaijan received promotions as well.[233]

On April 5, 1918, Enver Pasha approved the instructions on establishment, tasks, and activities of the Caucasus Army of Islam. According to the instructions, "the main purpose of establishment of the Caucasus Army of Islam was to lay the foundation of an army to be comprised of Caucasians, gradually

---

[232] W. E. D. Allen and P. Muratof, 1828-1921. *Türk-Kafkaz sınırındakı harpleri tarihi* [The Caucasian battlefields: A history of the wars on the Turko-Caucasian border 1828-1921] (Ankara, 1966), p. 401.

[233] N. Yucer, op. cit., p. 57.

expand this foundation, train the Caucasian soldiers, and secure the high values of Islam, and political and military ties with the Caliph of the Sacred Law and the Ottoman State."[234]

Nuri Pasha chose 149 officers and civil servants, 488 soldiers and sergeants from the Sixth Army for the foundation of the Caucasus Army of Islam. Groups of some 20-30 servicemen were sent to Azerbaijan in the beginning of April 1918.[235]

On May 9, after overcoming long and poor roads, a staff of 20 officers finally reached Tabriz. At that time, the majority of the territory of South Azerbaijan, including Tabriz, was under the Ottoman control. The local population of the county located nearby Lake Urmia was distressed by the Armenian military. Those who managed to survive appealed to the Turkish command for help. The Ottoman military command reacted swiftly and sent troops to aid the local population. When in Tabriz, Nuri Pasha assigned a special task to the officers to gather intelligence on the British troops zealous to invade Baku. Following the order, Ibrahim Kamal Bey began to collect information on the situation around the British troops withdrawing from Lake Urmia and met with the governor of the Gilan province, Kichik Khan, to discuss the prospects of joint activities of the Ottoman Army with the armed units of Kichik Khan.[236] Then on May 12, Nuri Pasha's mission moved on Savujbulag-Tebriz-Alajuje road and arrived at the Aras River on May 20. The officers crossed the river and

---

[234] Türk Silahlı Kuvvetleri Askeri Tarih ve Strateji Etüt Başkanlığı arşivi (ATASE) folder 1, file 1, sheet 19.

[235] Ibid., sheet 29-30.

[236] A.N. Kurat, op. cit., p. 385.

entered the Zangezur province of Azerbaijan where they were met triumphantly by the local population. When the group reached Zangezur, ferocities of the Armenian military against the Azerbaijani civilians were climaxing. Nuri Pasha kept several Turkish officers in the province with the purpose of preventing the Armenian aggression and organize resistance groups from the local people. Some other Turkish officers were dispatched to Nakhchivan and Ordubad.[237]

After Zangezur, Nuri Pasha proceeded to Yevlakh via Jabrayil, Aghdam, and Terter. Upon Nuri Pasha's arrival in Yevlakh on May 24, the residents greeted his mission with fervor. The Turkish commander initially chose to headquarter the Caucasus Army of Islam in Nukha (now Sheki), but he had to change his decision and established the headquarters in Ganja due to high activity of Armenian units around Nukha and the fact that the town was located aloof from the main transport routes. On May 25, Nuri Pasha arrived in Ganja and set to organizing resistance groups in several provinces. Within a short time, he set up a command post and formed smaller teams for the maintenance of law and order in Ganja, Gazakh, Zagatala, Nukha, Aghdam, Jabrayil, Karabakh, and the eastern territories of Zangezur. Prior to Nuri Pasha's arrival in Azerbaijan, guerilla groups had formed in different provinces of Azerbaijan to stand against the Armenian invaders. These units were led by formerly captive Turkish officers who had been taken to Azerbaijan from the front line. However, at that time, the Azerbaijani corps was very low on manpower. The entire military personnel included one thousand soldiers and

---

[237] N. Yucer, op. cit., p. 57.

officers, with half of them being former Turkish prisoners.[238] Under these circumstances, Nuri Pasha, already familiarized with the situation, was assured that without reinforcement, the Ottoman campaign in Azerbaijan would not yield any results.

Enver Pasha, apprised of the state of affairs in Azerbaijan, ordered the attachment of the Fifth Caucasus Division of the East Armies Group to the Caucasus Army of Islam. The Fifth Caucasus Division was manned with 257 officers and 5,575 men.[239] However, the active Ottoman forces dispatched to Azerbaijan were still fewer in number than the opposing Dashnak-Bolshevik troops. On June 20, 1918, Nuri Pasha sent a letter to Enver Pasha with a request for additional 20,000 rifles and ammunition; he also experienced shortage in qualified officers for organization of regular infantry and cavalry troops.[240] In view of these deficiencies and with the purpose to ensure the success of the Caucasus Campaign, Enver Pasha dispatched the Fifteenth Infantry Division with 157 officers and 7,636 men to be placed under the command of the Caucasus Army of Islam. The Fifteenth Infantry Division was commanded by Lieutenant Colonel Suleyman Izzet Bey.[241] Both the Fifth Caucasus Division and the Fifteenth Infantry Division were battle-hardened during WWI and were honored to bear the name of the most courageous divisions of the

---

[238] E. Rüştü, *Büyük harpda Bakü yollarında* [On the way to Baku during the Great War] (Ankara, 1934), p. 89.

[239] Ibid., p. 92.

[240] T. Sünbül, *Azerbaycan dosyası* [Azerbaijani file] (Ankara, 1980), p. 141.

[241] Ibid., p. 146.

Ottoman Army. In the subsequent correspondence, Nuri Pasha emphasized the numerical superiority of the opposing troops and convinced Enver Pasha to send reinforcements (the 106th and 107th regiments of the 36th Division). By comparison, the Baku Soviet troops numbered over 20,000 by the end of June 1918.[242]

The Turkish troops entered a fierce battle upon their arrival in Azerbaijan. The Bolshevik-Dashnak forces advanced westward both on Shamakhi road and by rail and launched an all-out attack on Ganja, the then capital of the Azerbaijani Democratic Republic. In the face of the Bolshevik-Dashnak threat, the command of the Caucasus Army of Islam decided to move troops eastward in order to block the adversary. Nuri Pasha identified the priority tasks: preventing the potential Armenian threat in and around Ganja, disarming Armenians in the city, and ensuring the security of the Azerbaijani population. By that time, over twenty thousand Armenians had settled in Ganja, predominantly in its eastern quarters. The Armenian community opposed the arrival of the Ottoman troops in Azerbaijan and stood against their intention to establish headquarters in Ganja. They were anxious to see the rapid advancement of the Baku Soviet forces toward Ganja. The local Armenians had formed an armed unit of six hundred men supplied with various weapons, including machine guns and ammunition. On June 10, Nuri Pasha ordered the disarmament of the Ganja Armenians. The next day, Nuri Pasha's Ganja unit surrounded the Armenian quarter;

---

[242] A. B. Kadishev, *Interventsiia i grazhdanskaia voina v Zakavkaz'e* [Intervention and civil war in Transcaucasia] (Moscow, 1960), p. 189.

the soldiers and officers of the Turkish cavalry regiment assumed prebattle positions and captured four Armenian watchmen. Two of the Ottoman officers went to the Armenian quarter to explain the necessity of surrendering their weapons. The Armenians refused to yield and fired at the officers. Then they attacked furiously, trying to surround the Turkish troops. Thirteen soldiers were killed and seven were wounded from the Turkish side in the clash. The Ganja unit retreated to take better-defended positions and eventually rebuffed the Armenian attack. The commander of the Turkish Army notified the Armenians through a German national from Helenendorf that if they chose to continue the hostilities, the Armenian district would be bombarded. After the warning, at 11:00 p.m., a priest, an Armenian officer, and a commissar holding a white flag appeared in front of the Ganja unit headquarters. After negotiations, the Armenians agreed to give up their arms. However, the Armenians failed to keep their promise again. The Turkish military command decided to suspend the operation till the next morning. On June 12, Turkish artillery forced the Armenians to surrender. The Ottoman troops kept the Armenian quarter in a blockade for three days and completed the process of disarming the Armenians.[243] Thus the potential threat for the Caucasus Army of Islam in Ganja was eliminated.

The arrival of the Turkish troops in Ganja by invitation of the Azerbaijani Democratic Republic, the buildup of the Caucasus Army of Islam under Nuri Pasha's command, and the shaping of the Azerbaijani National Army perturbed the leaders of the Baku Soviet of People's Commissars. On June 6, 1918,

---

[243] N. Keykurun, op. cit., p. 59.

the Baku Soviet forces with twenty thousand soldiers attacked westward from Hajigabul by the Order No. 8 of the commissar of war and navy affairs, Korganov, with an aim to terminate the activities of the Azerbaijani National Government in Ganja. The majority of the soldiers and the officers of this Red Army were ethnic Armenians; three of the four commissars leading the offensive were also Armenians. On June 6, before marching out to Ganja, Korganov addressed the personnel: "You must determine the fate of the peasants' and workers' revolution in Transcaucasia. If Turkish generals enter Baku with their troops, they will smash the Soviet rule. That's why you must defend the hub of the oil industry, Baku, for the Soviet republic. You will receive all necessary support from the North Caucasus."[244]

Initially, the Baku Soviet troops marched toward Ganja without encountering any resistance. On June 16, the Soviet army confronted the Army of Islam near the village of Gara-Maryam. At 9:00 a.m., the Soviet troops launched an assault on the opposing unit comprised of Azerbaijanis, Georgians, and Dagestanis. In the seven-hour-long battle, the Azerbaijani national troops tried to prevent the Soviet units from penetrating into Gara-Maryam but failed to fulfill the task. Gara-Maryam, which had an important strategic position, was captured by the Bolshevik-Dashnak forces.

The Baku Soviet military entered the Azerbaijani villages, took away all weapons from the people, and appropriated their food and pack animals. Any unarmed villagers who attempted to resist were killed without hesitation. At the same time, the

---

[244] Suren Shaumian, *Bakinskaia Kommuna* [The Baku commune] (Baku, 1927), p. 54.

Soviet command established special groups in the invaded villages to propagandize the population and organize an anti-Ottoman front. In order to strengthen the Red Army, the Bolsheviks announced a military draft of non-Muslims born between 1893 and 1897.

The course of the battle of Gara-Maryam was closely analyzed in the headquarters of the Caucasus Army of Islam. The commander of the Caucasus Army of Islam, Nuri Pasha, the commander of the Azerbaijani corps, Aliagha Shikhlinski, and the chief of staff of the Fifth Caucasus Division, Rüştü Bey, made a visit to the front line to study the situation from the ground, regroup the forces, and mobilize all resources. Nuri Pasha also visited Goychay and met not only with the soldiers but also with the local people; he called the villagers to render all possible aid to the Turkish-Azerbaijani troops.

After a thorough examination of the situation at the front line, Nuri Pasha put off doubts of the eventual victory over the Bolsheviks despite the failure in the first battle; he was assured that the joint Turkish-Azerbaijani troops could achieve a military advantage by mobilizing all available resources. Therefore, Nuri Pasha ordered preparation for a decisive battle and dispatched reinforcement to Goychay. The troops prepared their front line until June 27. On June 26, the Bolshevik-Dashnak forces obtained intelligence on the precombat preparations undertaken by the Caucasus Army of Islam. Upon receiving this information, the Red Army headquarters made a decision to attack without delay in order to forestall the Azerbaijani offensive and take the military initiative. The Baku Soviet troops launched an attack on June 27, but the Army of Islam held their ground. This was the first time when the Bolshevik detachments could not win a battle they had started. The unexpectedly launched battle had a great psychological importance for the Caucasus Army of Islam. The results of battle proved that the Bolshevik-Dashnak forces were not invincible and that a properly prearranged combat could halt the Bolsheviks and undermine their plans. In the early morning of June 29, the Caucasus Army of Islam pushed forward to a winning attack. The operational flexibility and swiftness of the headquarters of the Caucasus Army of Islam, timely reinforcement of the troops defending Goychay, and high morale among the Azerbaijani soldiers effectively neutralized the efforts of the Bolshevik forces led by Dashnak Amirov. The Bolsheviks, defeated near Goychay, were forced to retreat and took positions four miles off the town. On July 1, the Dashnak-Bolshevik units gave up and, when they saw no prospect for further advance, began to retreat.[245]

Thus, in the battles around Goychay and Gara-Maryam from mid-June to early July, the Caucasus Army of Islam achieved a sweeping victory over the joint Bolshevik-Dashnak troops and flung them back to Aghsu. The Bolshevik military could not take the military initiative again after these clashes. During that period, the Caucasus Army of Islam, joined by the Azerbaijani volunteers, achieved major progress in their conduct of combat, from a defeat in the early fight to a confident superiority after the battle of Goychay.

---

[245] Erdaş Nilgün. Milli *mücadile döneminde Kafkas Cümhuriyyetleri ilə ilişkiler (1917-1921)* [Relationships with the Republics of Caucausus at the time of the national struggle (1917-1921)] (Ankara, 1994), p. 39.

In parallel with the battles near Goychay, there were clashes between the Turkish-Azerbaijani troops and the Red Army along the Kura River near Salyan; the sides fought to gain control of this strategically important location. Salyan was considered to be a key to the rich grain stocks of the Mughan plain. The failure to capture a bridge over the Kura River near Yevlakh during the Ganja march impelled the Baku Soviet leaders and the command of the Bolshevik-Dashnak troops to seek other options. The Soviet leadership planned to send special troops on vessels from the Caspian Sea up the Kura River to Yevlakh to arrange the explosion of the Yevlakh bridge. From June 16 till July 2, Salyan turned into a battlefield for the Soviet military fighting against the Turkish-Azerbaijani troops. The Soviet units in Salyan included over two thousand infantry soldiers and held twelve machine guns, six cannons, two warships, and one troopship sailing in the Kura River. Although the Dashnak-Bolshevik units outnumbered the Muslim troops and were better equipped, on July 2, the latter rebuffed the Dashnak-Bolshevik assault and forced them to retreat.[246]

On July 5, the joint Turkish-Azerbaijani troops marched toward Aghsu. The next morning, they attacked and defeated the Dashnak-Bolshevik forces and drove them out of Aghsu. The Baku Soviet forces partially retreated southward and overran positions in Kurdemir.[247]

On July 7 and 8, 1918, the Turkish-Azerbaijani troops reached Kurdemir and immediately engaged in a battle. The military superiority of the Bolsheviks, who even possessed an

---

[246] N. Yucer, op. cit., p. 95.
[247] Ibid., p. 96.

ironclad train and armored vehicles, did not deter the Army of Islam. By the night of July 10, the Muslims proved able to push the Dashnak-Bolshevik units out of Kurdemir and began pursuit of the retreating troops.

Dislodgement of the Soviet troops from Shamakhi was the next task of the Caucasus Army of Islam on its way to Baku. Fighting for Shamakhi with its complex terrain became a serious challenge for the Muslim troops; the task, if completed successfully, would free the local population from the fear of the Armenian atrocities once for all. Shamakhi also had an important strategic location for further direct advancement toward Baku. For this reason, the command of the Caucasus Army of Islam deemed it essential to prepare extensively for a decisive assault on Shamakhi and complete it at the earliest time. On July 19, 1918, Mursel Pasha, the commander of the Eastern Front, ordered an attack on Shamakhi. Heavy rain and muddy roads complicated the movement of the weaponry in the mountains. Despite these difficulties, the soldiers of the Tenth and Thirteenth Regiments demonstrated physical endurance and delivered heavy strikes at the Soviet troops. In the afternoon, the Bolshevik-Dashnak detachments started a massive retreat back to Shamakhi.[248] The battle continued on July 20; by nightfall, the Bolshevik troops were dislodged from Shamakhi, and the Turkish-Azerbaijani forces took over the town. Anastas Mikoyan, one of the Baku Soviet leaders and the commissar of the third brigade in Shamakhi, accused the commander of the Third Army Hamazasp (Srvandztian) in failing to arrange proper defense of Shamakhi. The Baku

---

[248] E. Rüştü, op. cit., p. 149.

Soviet leadership sent urgent telegrams to Lenin and Stalin and dispatched reinforcement to support the Bolshevik-Dashnak troops; however, all efforts to recapture Shamakhi were doomed to failure.[249]

The Bolshevik-Dashnak forces attempted to take advantage of the temporary ceasefire on the front line. Chaos in the Red Army units ascended to the Baku Soviet and brought the entity to the verge of a collapse. The last resort of the Bolshevik leaders in Baku was an aid from Soviet Russia—their only ally capable of redressing the situation. By Lenin's direction, a well-armed Soviet unit of 780 soldiers led by Petrov was transferred to Baku from the Ukrainian Front. On July 19, Petrov arrived in Baku with his unit and was immediately appointed as the military commissar of the Baku district. It was clear that Petrov's unit by itself was incapable of preventing the march of the Caucasus Army of Islam to Baku. Under these circumstances, the Bolsheviks appealed to their supporters among the Baku residents and tried to attract additional military support to the Bolshevik-Dashnak detachments at the front line by appealing to chauvinistic sentiments of the non-Azerbaijani population.[250]

As the units of the Caucasus Army of Islam approached Baku, the political forces around the Baku Commissars became embroiled in contention. The leaders of the Baku Soviet,

---

[249] Suren Shaumian, op. cit., p. 69.

[250] E. A. Tokarzhevskii, *Iz istorii inostrannoi interventsii i qrazhdanskoi voiny v Azerbaijane* [Glimpses of history of the foreign intervention and the civil war in Azerbaijan] (Baku, 1957), pp. 190-191.

extraneous to the Azerbaijani nation, realized that in case of marching of the Muslim troops in Baku, they would be held liable for the tragedies and crimes they had committed. The only way out was seen in bringing the British troops to Baku. Some Baku Soviet members—the Socialist-Revolutionaries (SR) and the Dashnaks—reckoned that the advent of the British troops in Baku would keep the Caucasus Army of Islam out of the city and strengthen their positions in Baku. The Bolsheviks suffered a heavy defeat in an extraordinary meeting of the Baku Soviet on July 25. Despite all efforts of the Bolsheviks in the meeting, the right-wing SR, the Dashnaks, and the Mensheviks voted in favor of inviting British troops to Baku.[251]

The Turkish-Azerbaijani troops were rapidly approaching Baku without facing any serious resistance in the suburbs; the Muslim command cherished illusions for a prompt surrender of the city. On July 31, the commander of the Caucasus Army of Islam sent envoys to the Baku Soviet to persuade them to surrender peacefully and avoid unnecessary casualties. The Turkish-Azerbaijani command guaranteed a corridor for Armenians who chose to leave the city. Enver Pasha was personally in control of the surrender process; he ordered, by telegram, that all Armenians be in no way hindered from moving to Armenia, if they peacefully surrendered the city. The Armenians of Baku and their supporters expected that the early arrival of the British troops in Baku would change the state of affairs in their favor.[252]

---

[251] Ibid., p. 198.

[252] L. Dunsterville, *The Adventures of Dunsterforce* (London: Arnold, 1920), pp. 207-9. Russian translation: *Britanskii imperializm v*

On the night of July 30, the Bolsheviks made their last try to preserve their power. The Baku Soviet and the Dashnaktsutiun leaders made a common decision to send all remaining units to the front line. On August 1, the Socialist Revolutionaries, the Mensheviks, and the Armenians declared a new government in Baku—the Centrocaspian Dictatorship—dominated by the Dashnaktsutiun Party.[253]

The strife for power prompted the toppled Baku Soviet commissars to leave Baku for Astrakhan in quest of support from Bolshevik authorities consolidated there. The initial attempt failed, and on August 14, the former commissars were arrested by the Centrocaspian Dictatorship and convicted of embezzlement. A month later, on September 14, the commissars utilized the final offensive of the Caucasus Army of Islam and escaped from prison under heavy bombardment. They managed to board the vessel *Turkmen*, which initially set a course for Astrakhan. However, the commissars were exposed by the crew, and the vessel changed its course for Krasnovodsk where the commissars were surrendered to the Turkestan socialist-revolutionary government. The Turkestani government, which had received resolution of the Centrocaspian Dictatorship sentencing the commissars to death without investigation, supported the decision. On September 19, the commissars were shot dead in Agjakum valley.

In early August, the Caucasus Army of Islam continued marching toward Baku. On August 3, the Muslim troops

---

Baku i Persii v 1917-1918 g. [British imperialism in Baku and Persia in 1917-1918] (Tbilisi, 1925), p. 89.

[253] Ibid., p. 114.

ANAR ISGENDERLI

engaged in a battle with the Centrocaspian units between Khirdalan and Bilajari settlements northeast of Baku. After winning the battle, Mursel Pasha, the commander of the Eastern Front, resent his ultimatum to the forces in control of the city. The letter was written in the Russian and the Turkish languages and addressed to the chairman of the Armenian National Council in Baku and the commander of the Centrocaspian Army. The letter read,

> Mr. Chairman of the Armenian National Council, as you are aware, the Turkish Army is at the approaches to Baku. If you agree to surrender the city peacefully, I guarantee the protection of rights of everybody regardless of ethnicity and faith. If the city is not surrendered, you will be responsible for bloodshed and losses sustained after occupation of the city.[254]

The leaders of the Armenian National Council and the Dashnaktsutiun Party left the ultimatum unanswered and resumed fighting against the Turkish-Azerbaijani troops.

On August 4, a small detachment of the British troops, headed by Colonel Stokes, arrived in Baku. The British military assistance, moderate as it was, enheartened the leaders of the Centrocaspian Dictatorship and gave a second wind to the Dashnak troops. The leaders of the Centrocaspian Dictatorship propagandized the residents and tried to assure the population by alleging that the British command would

---

[254] *Kut'ül Amare Kahramanı Halil Paşa'nın Anıları: Bitmeyen Savaş* (Istanbul, 1972), p. 213.

send thirty thousand troops against the Turkish Army. The propaganda yielded results.

The Turkish army planned to launch a decisive attack on Baku on August 5. The battle began early in the morning with the Caucasus Army of Islam taking the initiative. The Muslims prevailed all along the line of contact. The Centrocaspian troops retreated after the first thrust of the Muslims. The Dashnak defense line, which lay through the Bayil hights and the hills of Gurd Gapsy, was captured by the Caucasus Army of Islam. However, despite the penetration through the outer line of resistance and approach to the second defense line, the attack halted due to an insufficient supply of artillery shells. The Muslim infantry, left without artillery support, was forced to take up defensive dispositions. The situation reversed—the Dashnaks flung the Muslim units three miles back. The death toll among the Dashnak-Centrocaspian forces reached 2,000. The Caucasus Army of Islam lost 139 soldiers and 9 officers, and 463 Muslim servicemen were injured in the combat.[255]

The failure of the Muslim army to gain control over Baku reanimated the Dashnaks. On August 6, after reinforcement of the Armenian-Russian units by the British detachment of General Dunsterville,[256] all able men of Baku aged between sixteen and sixty-five were compulsively drafted into the army. Some six hundred Muslims who resisted the order were immediately executed.[257]

---

[255] N. Yucer, op. cit., p. 120.

[256] Dunsterville, op. cit., pp. 218-317.

[257] M. Saray, *Azerbaycan türkleri tarihi* [History of Azerbaijani Turks] (Istanbul, 1993), pp.122-123.

Successful completion of the Muslim offensive required substantial reinforcement by the local troops and, above all, heightening of the morale among the soldiers and revival of the winning spirit. With this aim in mind, a few days later, the command of the Caucasus Army of Islam addressed to the soldiers:

> To the Turkish Army! If you do not capture this city of treasure and gold, you will miss an opportunity to make a precious gift to our beloved motherland. If you do not capture the famous city near the green sea, you will see the Caucasian Turks and the Muslims of Turkestan stabbed in the heart with a poisoned dagger with the following words engraved on it: 'Alas, the Turks did not come to our relief.' The Caucasus will wail and Turkestan will lament."

The liberation of Baku was a critical cause for the Azerbaijanis, who saw it as the future capital of an independent Azerbaijan. Rasulzade, while in Turkey, wrote in a letter to the minister of foreign affairs, M. Hajinski: "Baku must be seized soon by all means and at any cost. Otherwise we will achieve a stalemate. Should we fail to overtake Baku, it will be all over. Then good-bye, Azerbaijan!"[258]

The battle of August 5 was followed by a brief truce. The Centrocaspian and the British troops attempted to take advantage of the opportunity and press the success but were repulsed by the Turkish troops. Meanwhile, within

---

[258] SARA, col. 894, list 10, file 154, sheet 16.

a few days, the Caucasus Army of Islam took control of Novkhany, Goradil, Pirshaghy, Kurdekhany, and Fatmai villages and drew the villagers of Mashtagha and Hokumeli into the units attacking Baku. Protracted battles from August 25 to September 13 ended with the predominance of the Turkish-Azerbaijani troops, which drew closer to Baku.[259] On September 14, at half past eight in the evening, the commander of the Caucasus Army of Islam, Nuri Pasha, issued Order No. 100 to launch the final assault on the city. The number of soldiers and officers was increased up to fourteen thousand, including eight thousand Ottomans and six thousand Azerbaijanis.[260]

On September 15, at 5:30 a.m., the Muslim troops mounted a crucial offensive. The leadership of the Centrocaspian Dictatorship, realizing the hopelessness of the situation and its inability to repulse the attack, agreed to begin talks. At 10:30 a.m., the commander of the Western Front of the Centrocaspian Army arrived at the headquarters of the Fifth Muslim Division in a car with a white flag aloft.[261] He accepted an ultimatum of unconditional surrender on the following terms:

1. Capitulation of troops in the city
2. Surrender of artillery, other arms, and buildings
3. Release of Turkish, German, and Austrian prisoners from their imprisonment on Nargin Island

---

[259] N. Yucer, op. cit., p. 137.
[260] W. E. D. Allen and P. Muratof, op. cit., p. 458.
[261] E. Rüştü, op. cit., p. 212.

4. Surrender of ammunition depots, food, trucks, armored
   vehicles, planes, and other military equipment[262]

In the fights for Baku, the Turkish-Azerbaijani army captured 17 Armenian and 9 Russian officers and 1,151 Armenian, 383 Russian, 4 British, and 113 other soldiers. The Fifth Muslim Division lost up to 1,130 servicemen in the battles for Baku from early August till mid-September. The overall death toll among the Muslim officers and soldiers perished in the battles for the independence of Azerbaijan exceeded 4,000 from mid-June till mid-September, not including casualties in the voluntary Azerbaijani units.[263]

Thus, on September 15, at 3:00 p.m., Baku was completely taken under the control of the Caucasus Army of Islam. Nuri Pasha sent congratulatory telegrams to the Ottoman minister of war, Enver Pasha, and to the Azerbaijani Government in Ganja. Nuri Pasha also requested the Azerbaijani Government to swiftly dispatch a police force from Ganja to establish and preserve order in Baku. The establishment of Turkish control over Baku brought about rejoicing both within the Azerbaijani society and among the leaders of the Ottoman Empire, especially Enver Pasha. Rasulzade wrote of that historical moment: "September 15 is as valuable as May 28 in the history of the Azerbaijani nation. On May 28 the independence of the

---

[262] Süleyman İzzet, *Birinci Dünya Harbi'nde Azerbaycan ve Dağıstan Muharebelerinde 15-ci Piyade Tümeni*, [15th Infantry Division's movements and battles in Azerbaijan and North Caucasia in WWI] (Ankara, 1936), p. 49.

[263] Süleyman İzzet, op. cit., p. 49.

Republic was declared to the world, whereas on September 15 this independence gained a solid foundation. With liberation of Baku by the Caucasus Army of Islam the head joined the body. Baku is the head and the body is Azerbaijan."[264]

Fatali Khan Khoyski, the then prime minister of Azerbaijan, wrote to Nuri Pasha on the occasion of taking control of Baku: "On behalf of my nation I am proud to enunciate our gratitude to the bravest and noblest soldiers in the world—the sons of the Turkish people on the occasion of liberating Baku, the capital of Azerbaijan, from the enemies. The nation is grateful to you."[265]

The commanders of the Turkish Army—Nuri Pasha, Halil Pasha, Mursel Pasha, and others—were hosted by the esteemed "father of the people," a great enlightener and patron, Haji Zeynal-Abdin Taghiyev. Taghiyev, who had promised to present his grand double-story mansion (now the Museum of the Azerbaijani History) to the Turkish command in case of their triumph and liberation of Baku, kept his pledge and placed the building at the service of the Turkish officers.[266]

A few days after entering Baku, the Caucasus Army of Islam began to prepare a mission for Karabakh to prevent the massacre of Azerbaijanis launched by the Dashnak gangs. Some other unit of the Army continued the rescue campaign toward Dagestan.

---

[264] *Azerbaycan* journal (July-October 1993): p. 80.

[265] *Azerbaycan* journal issue no. 7 (1962): p. 29.

[266] Onk Nizamettin, "Yeni Azerbaycan kurularken" ["While building new Azerbaijan"], *Türk Dünyası* journal of history (April 1992): p. 34.

4.4. The Baku Soviet of People's Commissars

The slaughters of the Turkic population in March 1918, launched by Dashnak Armenian gangs under the guidance of Stepan Shaumian, altered the political situation in Baku in the favor of Bolsheviks. Most of the Azerbaijani families had to leave the city; many of them fled to Central Asia and Persia, and the rest scattered in the surrounding villages to escape genocide by the Bolshevik-Dashnak gangs. Patronized by high-ranking Armenian "Bolsheviks," the Dashnaktsutiun leaders acted as sole owners of Baku. All papers and magazines but Armenian-Bolshevik political organs were shut down. Bolsheviks gained control of the entire transport and established a labor commissariat and food directorate. Notwithstanding the ban on all national councils, the Armenian National Council continued functioning.

On April 25, Bolsheviks established the Baku Soviet of People's Commissars to assume the entire authority over the city. After being elected the Baku Soviet's chairman, Shaumian, under the veil of establishment of "workers' and peasants' authority," set a goal to cleanse Azerbaijan of Azerbaijanis, plunder the resources of the country, and realize the dream of Great Armenia on the Azerbaijani lands. Following Shaumian's order of April 26, Bolsheviks stripped fifty million manats from local bourgeoisie by using force and intimidation. The money, violently reived from Azerbaijani magnates, was later found in Shaumian's cabin when he attempted to flee from Baku.

Under Russian guidance, Shaumian nationalized the oil industry and arranged the delivery of oil to Russia. In order to speed up the production and transportation of the Azerbaijani oil, Lenin approved allocation of one hundred million rubles to the Baku Soviet. In comparison with the period between November 1917 and March 1918, when only 4,313,000 *puds* of oil were delivered to Russian ports, this number increased drastically and reached 80,025,000 *puds* from early April to late July 1918. Over 700,000 *puds* of cotton, 100,000 *puds* of dried fish, tons of rice, salt, and other provisions were supplied to Russia from Baku and Azerbaijani provinces under the guise of fraternal aid.[267]

The Baku Soviet dismissed the city *duma* of Baku chaired by Fatali Khan Khoyski and declared the Transcaucasian Seim a counterrevolutionary entity. The Moscow leadership applied best efforts to bolster the Baku Soviet both in military and political terms. At Lenin's direction, the Military Commissariat and the Council for Revolutionary Struggle arranged swift supply of all necessary ammunition for the Dashnak-Bolshevik troops in Baku and sent five thousand rifles, two million cartridges, thirty-five machine guns, four armored vehicles, and thirteen aircrafts.[268] Grigory Korganov, then navy commissar of the Baku Soviet, writes in a letter to Moscow: "The commune army numbers 18,000 troops; the overall majority of soldiers, roughly 13,000, and almost all officers are Armenians."[269] The commanders of the Baku Soviet troops—Z. Avetisian, N.

---

[267] *Azərbaycanda sosialist inqilabının qələbəsi uğrunda bolşeviklərin mübarizəsi. Sənədlər və materiallar. 1917-1918* [Bolsheviks' struggle for the victory of socialist revolution in Azerbaijan. Documents and records. 1917-1918] (Baku, 1960), p. 89.

[268] Ibid., p. 191.

[269] Suren Shaumian, op. cit., p. 25.

Ghazarian, and Amazasp Srvantstian—were former gangsters, notorious for outrageous atrocities against Azerbaijanis. The Baku Soviet's leader Shaumian, unable to reach Nakhchivan directly, dispatched his directives to Andranik, whose ferocious gang terrorized the Azerbaijani population in the region. In July 1918, Andranik wired to Shaumian: "Julfa is in hand. It is at your disposal."[270] To that end, in July 1918, Andranik announced the establishment of the Bolshevik rule in Nakhchivan and declared the province an integral part of Soviet Russia. On June 4, 1918, Andranik telegraphed Shaumian, asserting his readiness to render obedience and accept the authority of the central Russian government and help the Baku Commune. After reporting the news to Lenin, Shaumian replied by wire: "Julfa, to people's leader Andranik. I have received your telegram no. 577 and passed the full text to the central government in Moscow. For our part, I greet you as a true hero of the people."[271] Further in the telegram, Shaumian requested to politicize the Armenian aggression and seek access routes to Baku.

One of the primary goals of the Baku Soviet was establishment of the Dashnak-Bolshevik rule in Azerbaijani provinces through massacres and genocide of Azerbaijani Turks. The Baku Soviet, hostile to the idea of national sovereignty of Azerbaijan, was prepared to rather burn Baku than cede it to the Azerbaijani Democratic Republic. The time-dictated

---

[270] Ch. Agaian, *Rol' Rossii v istoricheskikh sud'bakh armianskogo naroda* [Russia's role in the historic foredoom of the Armenian people] (Moscow, 1978), p. 267.

[271] Ch. Agaian, op. cit., p. 260.

overturn of the alien anti-Azerbaijani regime became a sacred duty of the national government of Azerbaijan.

4.5. The British Troops Enter Baku

The political developments in Azerbaijan hinged on twists and consequences of the world-shaking war rather than domestic processes. In the imperialist war between the two belligerent camps, Azerbaijan naturally supported the Ottomans and hoped for their victory to secure its own interests. However, the events took a different course. On October 30, 1918, Turkey signed the Mudros Treaty with the Entente. The treaty obligated the defeated Ottoman troops to withdraw from Baku, desist from impeding the occupation of Baku by the Entente troops, and yield the control over Transcaucasian railroad to the Entente. The British detachments disembarking from the Persian port of Anzali were to occupy Baku on behalf of the allies. Article 11 of the Mudros Treaty declared Azerbaijan within the circle of British influence, whereas Article 15 stipulated British control over roads and oilfields of Azerbaijan and enforced Turkey to refrain from protesting against occupation of Baku. Azerbaijan's plenipotentiary representative in the Ottoman Empire, Alimerdan Topchubashov, voiced his government's concern in regard to the severe conditions of the Mudros Treaty, which affected Azerbaijan, and lodged an objection against the inclusion of clauses related to Baku and the Azerbaijani railroad in the treaty without Azerbaijan's participation. The note of protest emphasized that despite the recognition of the Azerbaijani Democratic Republic by the Ottoman government, it neglected the international law and regulations by accepting the clauses, which concern the capital city of Azerbaijan, and supporting British intervention in the country.[272] However, the Azerbaijani government fully realized its complete disability to influence the provisions of the treaty and, hence, dispatched a delegation to Anzali to settle relations with the British forces bound for Baku. In the meeting with General Thomson, the commander of the British forces in Anzali, the Azerbaijani envoys proposed that the British military command declared recognition of ADR prior to entering its territory. However, the proposal was rejected by General Thomson, who stated, "To my knowledge, the Azerbaijani people do not have a republic established by popular vote, there is only a government set up by the Turkish command. Nevertheless, if you claim the opposite, we shall check everything on the ground and make an appropriate decision. The Allies came in not to destruct, but to create."[273]

General Thomson declared that the Azerbaijani and the Turkish troops must withdraw from Baku before 10:00 a.m. on November 17. The British forces would take charge of Baku and its oilfields, and the rest of the country would stay under control of the Azerbaijani government and army. The manifesto refused to officially recognize Azerbaijan but provided for establishment of de facto relations between its government and envoys from the United Kingdom, France, and the United States and announced that all agencies and services would continue functioning with some adjustments. Other provisions implied

---

[272] SARA, col. 970, list 1, file 68, sheet 2.

[273] M. Mammadzade, *Milli Azərbaycan hərəkatı* [The Azerbaijani national movement] (Berlin, 1938; reprinted: Baku, 1992), p 107.

the appointment of General Thomson in the position of governor-general of Baku, establishment of British supervision over the city police, resumption of free functioning of the city *duma*, participation of Azerbaijani delegates in the Paris Peace Conference in accordance with the principle of national self-determination, entry of Lazar Bicherakhov and his troops along with the British forces in Baku, and debarment of the armed Armenian gangs in Baku.[274]

The talks of the Azerbaijani delegation with General Thomson had a certain success, mainly due to the stipulation of Azerbaijanis partaking in the peace conference and the obligation assumed by General Thomson to bar Armenian gangs from the city. The arrival of the British forces in Baku on November 17 entailed different attitudes from the local residents. Supporters of the Russian and the Armenian national councils rejoiced. Bicherakhov scattered leaflets from planes addressed "to the Russian Citizens," congratulating the Christian population of Baku for "embracing the Motherland." General Thomson's manifest, followed two days later, was in the same vein. However, his intentions were overshadowed by General Bicherakhov who announced the setup of the illegitimate Caucasian-Caspian government and launched preparations for a takeover in Baku. With Bicherakhov's arrival, rumormongers within the Armenian and the Russian national councils in Baku claimed that no Azerbaijani state existed, and there was one and undivided Russia. The Azerbaijani government was planned to be deposed and replaced by Bicherakhov's Caucasian-Caspian government.

---

[274] A. Ziyadxanlı, *Azərbaycan* (Baku, 1919; reprinted: Baku, 1993), p. 46.

Upon arrival in Baku, General Thomson met with representatives of local national and political groups, including delegates from Armenian and Azerbaijani communities of the town. He described these meetings and briefly characterized the situation in Baku in a report to his command:

> On the 18th [of November] . . . the Armenian Bishop called and poured forth some of the woes of his people and a "moderate" Armenian leader with him explained exactly which people, Russian and Tartar [i.e., Azerbaijanis], should be drastically dealt with, in his view, as a foundation to any building up process . . .
>
> Mr. Asadalieff[275] called by request and was most encouraging as to the prospects of forming a coalition provincial Government of moderates of all parties, politicians to be rigidly excluded. He is a very wealthy Tartar and carries much weight with all classes in consequence and apparently has been a moderating influence for many years . . .
>
> To form a hasty opinion of a complex situation with 72 hours experience is absurd. The following stand out as salient features:
>
> 1. National patriotism for a Great Russia whether a Monarchy or Republic is practically non-existent in Baku.

---

[275] Mirza Asadullayev, member of the National Council and future member of the Cabinet.

2. The hatred and intolerance between the uneducated Armenian and Tartar is incredible in its ferocity.

3. The educated Russian has lost heart at any rate temporarily, and carries little weight but he sides with the Tartar rather than the Armenian whom all stigmatise traitors to every cause they have supported from Bolshevism to the British.

4. The Allies are suspected of trying to push the Caucasus peoples under a Central Russian Government of some kind after making good terms for the British, French, and American pets, the Armenians.[276]

4.6. Forming the Azerbaijani Parliament

The Azerbaijani National Council, forced to cease activities on June 17, 1918, in Ganja, resumed its functions on November 16 in Baku. In the opening speech, Rasulzade declared, "Our National Council is not a council founded upon a constituent assembly and elected by popular vote. Our present National Council shall expand into a parliament and include representatives of all nations, who bind the fate of all strata of their societies with the fate of Azerbaijan, who rejoice at success and grieve over sorrows of Azerbaijan. Then we will have a

---

[276] Situation on arrival in Transcaucasia. Narrative of first few days in Baku. November 17-24, 1918, by Major General W. M. Thomson, commanding Northern Persian Force. The British Archives 6480105, CAB 45/107, pp. 2, 3, 5.

ANAR ISGENDERLI

full-fledged parliament."[277] The chairman of the government, F. Khoyski, addressed the council with a request to take charge of preparations for convening a constituting assembly due to the overwhelming workload of the government. Khoyski's request was agreed to by the Council.

On November 20, 1918, the second gathering of the national council in Baku, under the chairmanship of Rasulzade, brought an extensive discussion of the draft law on Forming an Interim Parliament of Azerbaijan. It should be noted that in late 1917, the Muslim parties of the South Caucasus contested in the elections to the Russian Constituent Assembly and won fourteen seats. Unable to participate in the Russian Constituent Assembly, they decided to form the Transcaucasian Commissariat in Tiflis, which included Azerbaijani, Georgian, and Armenian delegates. The fourteen Muslim deputies, elected through popular elections, managed to raise the number of seats to forty-four by virtue of the votes they gained. Unable to call a constitutive meeting in Azerbaijan, the Central Muslim Committee of the South Caucasus opted for representation of Azerbaijan in the Transcaucasian Seim in the interim.[278] The fourteen deputies who won in the elections to the Russian Constituent Assembly had come from various political movements and gained over one million of Muslim votes. Therefore, after self-termination of the Transcaucasian Seim on May 26, 1918, the forty-four Muslim deputies formed the Azerbaijani National Council and took charge of governance in Azerbaijan.

---

[277] SARA, col. 895, list 1, file 11, sheet 15.
[278] SARA, col. 894, list 10, file 187, sheets 1-2.

The meeting of the national council on November 20 recognized the fact that Azerbaijanis were not the only people living in Azerbaijan and emphasized the need for the council to represent all the minorities. At that time, none of the forty-four members of the council came from a minority. The orators noted that, along with political representation, the council should also include representatives of all social strata. The resolution on establishment of a parliament in Azerbaijan delimited the territory of the country, which included the Baku and the Ganja *guberniyas*, Zagatala *okrug*, parts of the Erivan and the Tiflis *guberniyas*. According to the Caucasus Almanac, the population of that territory was 2,750,000 people, including 1,900,000 Muslims, 500,000 Armenians, and 230,000 Russians. In terms of one representative per 24,000 people, the council resolved to grant eighty seats to Muslims, twenty-one seats to Armenians, ten seats to Russians, and one seat for German, Jewish, Georgian, and Polish minorities. The act implied direct transfer of the forty-four council members to the parliament as they had already been elected by popular vote. The remaining thirty-six seats were distributed among cities and *uyezds*.[279] The act also affirmed suffrage for both genders and all people within the borders of the country and hence made Azerbaijan the first country in the Orient to grant suffrage to women.

The twenty-one seats designated for Armenians were to be taken by members of the Armenian National Council from Ganja (eight seats), Shusha (eight seats), and Baku (five

---

[279] SARA, col. 895, list 3, file 187, sheets 1-2.

seats). Ten representatives of the Russian population were to be nominated by the Russian National Council.[280]

After gaining a foothold in Baku, General Thomson engaged in mounting a campaign of czarist Russia's ally—Great Britain—against Soviet Russia and rendered full support to armies of Denikin, Kolchak, and Yudenich. Thomson raised a demand against the government of Azerbaijan to establish earnest relationships with the Russian National Council, which, in its turn, demanded from the Azerbaijani government the recognition of Russia's territorial integrity, authority of the Russian Constituent Assembly, and Kolchak's government in Ufa. These issues were discussed in a closed meeting of the Azerbaijani National Council held in the evening of November 24. Speaking of the Russian demands, Khoyski noted that although it could be acceptable to recognize the Russian Constituent Assembly, Azerbaijan's vital aspiration was to send a delegation to the Paris Peace Conference concerned with consequences of World War I. He viewed the recognition of Kolchak's government unacceptable since it was not clear how the government was formed and who was in that government.[281]

After intense debates, the council made the following decisions:

1. The political situation and system in Azerbaijan to be sealed at the Paris Peace Conference.
2. The actual system of governance continues to stay in place.

---

[280] SARA, col. 895, list 3, file 25, sheets 3-5.
[281] SARA, col. 895, list 1, file 11, sheets 10-11.

3. If the Russian Constituent Assembly participates in the Paris Peace Conference along with representatives of all self-determined nations, Azerbaijan will join the conference as well to lobby its position on the issue of self-determination.[282]

The national council called its last meeting under chairmanship of Rasulzade at 8:00 p.m. on December 3, 1918. The chairman of the cabinet, Khoyski, conveyed the essence of the letter he had received at 2:00 p.m. that day from General Thomson. In his letter, Thomson declared that the parliament should not hold any session in Baku prior to establishment of a coalition government.[283]

Khoyski informed the council members of the cabinet's steps taken in regard to the letter and negotiations with Thomson. He also announced that besides Russians and Armenians, some Muslim groups also tried to drag the Azerbaijani National Council in the mud and persuade Thomson of its incompetence. Speaking of the negotiations with Thomson, Khoyski noted that he had insisted on the principle of a parliament-formed cabinet and had argued that a government should be established by the legislative authority elected by the majority of the population in order to rely on its support and be accountable to the parliament. Through long debates, Khoyski had managed to convince Thomson. Composition of the coalition government had been the second issue in the agenda of negotiations. Thomson had contended that the

---

[282] Ibid., sheets 11-12.
[283] Ibid., sheets 1-3.

government should include five representavies of the Mulsim population and five members for the Christian minority (three Russian and two Armenian members). In response, Khoyski had noted that Thomson's proposal was unfair to Muslims, who constituted an absolute majority of the population, and had made a counterproposal to compose the government of seven Azerbaijanis, three Armenians, and two Russians, or eight Azerbaijanis, three Armenians, and three Russians. Eventually, Khoyski convinced Thomson to accept the latter option. Finishing the narrative, the Premier stated that Thomson had assured him that he would support the functioning of the parliament and prevent any provoking incident on the opening day.

The first meeting of Khoyski with Thomson on November 20 was contentious. General Thomson declared that he did not recognize the Azerbaijani Democratic Republic and had come to the land of allied Russia. Khoyski responded that the establishment of the Republic was derived from commitment and aspiration of the Azerbaijani people and had been announced to the international community. Khoyski continued, "You [the British] are a great and also civilized nation and empire. You should accept our independence." The general responded, "These are political issues between the two countries. I am merely a soldier." Khoyski insisted, "If you are a soldier, then I am the Prime Minister of the Republic of Azerbaijan, which proclaimed its independence. We did not invite you here. I demand your withdrawal from my homeland." General Thomson replied through the translator, "Please tell His Excellency Prime Minister, that one should possess a military force in order to demand withdrawal of troops. As far as I know, your republic did not form an army." Khoyski returned, "Please tell His Excellency General that he possesses only military knowledge. He is either unaware of popular will or confuses us with Indians. We, the Azerbaijani Turks, had expelled over 100,000 Russian soldiers with the might of people beyond our borders before declaring independence. If you persist, it would take only few hours to throw a handful of British soldiers into the sea with the strength of people. But we neither expect malice from you, no bear you any malice."[284]

General Thomson provided his own accunt of the meeting with Premier Khoyski: "November 20th. The President [referring to Fatali Khan Khoyski] of Azerbaijan Government came with Mr. Assadalieff [i.e., Mirza Asadullayev] and explained at great length how the Republic were forced by circumstances into the arms of the Turks. He contended that he was glad to see them go and honestly welcomed the Allies as the hope for small nations. They look forward to complete emancipation from Russia and to that end were raising a 'defensive army' of 50,000 men. He acquiesced in the view that the representation of all parties in the Government was desirable and promised a reorganization on this basis within a fortnight. He clearly understands that the Allies have no intention of recognizing Independent Republics, and that all questions of that nature will be settled at the Peace Conference. He has little hope of a coalition Government but will give it a fair trial and will strive for justice for all. He asks that we should judge as to who will be

---

[284] N. Sheykhzamanli, *Azerbaycan istiqlal mücadelesi xatiralari* [Memoirs of the struggle for independence in Azerbaijan] (Baku, 1997), p. 85.

ANAR ISGENDERLI

the transgressor. He spoke bitterly of Russian Government and of the treachery of the Armenians, he admits that there is blame on all parties. Undoubtedly a clever man, a lawyer, who has set up a vigorous local administration, vastly more practicable than any previously known in the Caucasus. He stated round Nuri's having lingered and expressed indignation at his claiming to be in the employ of Azerbaijan. He would write and stop it and declared that all Turks either had gone or were on the point of doing so. The Azerbaijan Army had been removed from Baku as demanded by us, and would only be maintained at Elizabetpol and outlying districts against Armenian marauders commanded by Andronik and Avetissoff who were at the moment murdering Tartars in large numbers."[285]

On December 7, 1918, the Taghiyev Girl's School hosted the opening session of the Azerbaijani parliament. This was the first parliament formed on the utmost democratic principles of that time in the entire Muslim East. The parliament included representatives of all nationalities populating the country. The chairman of the national council, Rasulzade, made an extensive congratulatory address at the opening ceremony. By the nomination of the Musavat Party, Alimerdan Topchubashov was elected chairman *in absentia* (he was visiting Istanbul). Hasan Aghayev became his first deputy. Rahim Vakilov was confirmed in the office of Secretary of the Parliament. In Topchubashov's absence, the parliament was chaired by Hasan

---

[285] Situation on arrival in Transcaucasia. Narrative of first few days in Baku. November 17-24, 1918, by Major General W. M. Thomson, commanding Northern Persian Force. The British Archives 6480105, CAB 45/107, pp. 4-5.

Aghayev. The opening session of the parliament accepted the resignation of the cabinet and reassigned Fatali Khan Khoyski to form a new cabinet.[286]

4.7. The Government's Foreign and Domestic Policies

On December 26, 1918, Khoyski submitted a new list of ministers for parliamentary discussions. The parliament approved the program of the new cabinet and voted confidence in the government. Khoyski offered three ministerial posts to Russians and two portfolios to Armenians in his coalition government. Having witnessed the popular support of the government, General Thomson declared on December 28 the recognition of Khoyski's government as the only legal governing authority in Azerbaijan.

After the disclosure of the coup attempt plotted by Bicherakhov's group, General Thomson, upon demand of the Azerbaijani government, outlawed the Caucasus-Caspian government, dislodged them from Baku within forty-eight hours, and disarmed the Armenian detachments.

From December 1918, the British command gradually eased the restrictions imposed in Baku and lifted control over the Azerbaijani police, water transport, oil industry, financial system, and printed press. In April 1919, due to abolition of the British governorate in Baku, the first Azerbaijani regiment

---

[286] *Azərbaycan Xalq Cümhuriyyəti (1918-1920). Parlament* [The People's Republic of Azerbaijan (1918-1920). Parliament] volume 1 (Baku, 1998), p. 13.

formed in Ganja entered the capital and was gleefully received by the people.

This interim period was supposed to last till resolution of political issues concerning the Caucasus in the Paris Peace Conference. In February 1919, three months after the occupation of Baku by British troops, the Lloyd George government decided to withdraw the troops from the South Caucasus.[287] At the same time, strengthening of American or French influence in the region was not desirable for the British government, which proposed dislocation of the Italian army in the Caucasus. However, there was no agreement of opinion among the British political quarters on possibility of sending sufficient amount of Italian troops through the port of Batum. Lord Curzon, acknowledged as an expert in the regional issues, noted in a letter to Foreign Minister Arthur Balfour that military expansion in the Caucasus contradicts "national interests" of the Italians, who would not be able to stand long against encroaching Bolshevism.[288] Curzon's opinion remained disregarded, and on April 9, 1919, the British Military Council approved the British-Italian Treaty. On May 10, 1919, the British command notified the governments of Azerbaijan and Georgia of the decision of the British Military Council to remove troops from the South Caucasus.[289] The decision

---

[287] Tadeusz Swietochowski, *Russian Azerbaijan, 1905-1920: The Shaping of National Identity in a Muslim Community* (Cambridge, 1985; Turkish translation: Ankara, 1988), page 156.

[288] H. Nicolson, *Peacemaking 1919*, 1933, Russian translation (Moscow, 1945), p. 268.

[289] SARA, col. 970, list 1, file 54, sheet 11.

was an unexpected one for the commander of Allied Forces in Baku, General Thomson, who argued that "withdrawal of the British troops from the South Caucasus is an act of violence and betrayal of the newly established republics."[290]

At the end of June, delegates to the Paris Peace Conference from Azerbaijan and Georgia met with Louis Mallet, one of the chiefs of the British delegation, to express their concern about the withdrawal of British troops from the South Caucasus. Mallet confirmed the decision and responded that the troops were required in another region. He assured that Denikin's army would not enter neither Azerbaijan nor Georgia as the army's command had been respectively instructed by the newly appointed British high commissioner in the Caucasus, Wardrop.[291]

On June 28, the British delegation officially presented the decision to remove troops from the Caucasus to the Peace Conference. The decision prompted the Azerbaijani, Georgian, and mountaineer delegations to start negotiations with the Italians. However, the new Italian cabinet of Francesco Nitti suspended the issue of sending troops to the Caucasus, and the negotiations stalled.

In conformity with resolutions of the Paris Peace Conference, the British army undertook withdrawal starting from April 1919 and completely left the Caucasus by mid-August 1919. The government of Azerbaijan had not only managed to assert its power in the face of the British intervention but had also succeeded to gradually put the British command out of

---

[290] Tadeusz Swietochowski, op. cit., page 156.
[291] SARA, col. 970, list 1, file 142, sheet 19.

control over the city. However, although on the one part, the British withdrawal from Baku bolstered the independence of Azerbaijan, on the other part, it strengthened the desire of the Soviet Russian leadership to reinstate the foregone imperial borders. On August 23, 1919, British General Digby Inglis Shuttleworth addressed the residents of Baku on behalf of the Allied Command on the occasion of withdrawal of forces. The address read, "Taking this chance, we ask pardon for the departing British troops from the people of Azerbaijan, and especially from the population of Baku. We sincerely regret to say good-bye to our numerous friends and acquaintances, we wish them peace and happiness with all our hearts. All servicemen of the British army leave with their best memories of the days spent in Baku."[292]

After withdrawal of the British troops from Baku, General Shuttleworth wrote a report on the situation and the activity of the British command in Azerbaijan where he also touched upon the question of intercommunity relations in Baku between Azerbaijanis and Armenians:

It was evident that the Tartars . . . still believed that we should establish peace conditions. On the other hand the Russians and Armenians, who had accompanied us, were rather naturally thirsting for revenge. Consequently, when it became known that the British intended to work through the existing Government until such time as a new Government, representative of all classes, could be formed, a storm

---

[292] SARA, col. 970, list 1, file 144, sheet 9.

of indignation arose amongst our disappointed friends who had expected us to keep the ring while they paid off old scores. The population of Baku, at the time of re-occupation, consisted of some two hundred and sixty thousand souls, of whom two hundred thousand were Tartars. In Azerbaijan itself there was said to be a population of some four million of whoum three-fifths were Tartars the remainder being Armenians and Russians. There was a parliament sitting which consisted of members nominated on a proportionate basis by the various national councils and district associations, as constituted in pre-war days. The Armenians and Russians had been allotted a limited number of seats in this parliament . . .

It is interesting to observe that the Tartars stated that in former years no Mussulman apprentices were allowed by the Russians to learn how to become skilled workmen on the railways. It is a fact that each of our men trained some six Mussulman boys during our then months occupation of Baku, and reported very favourably upon their capacity and intelligence . . .

It will be remembered that General Bicherakov's Russian troops accompanied us to Baku while the Armenian troops were left at Lenkoran. Once the British were established in Baku the repartiation fo Russians and Armenians took place, with the result that the bulk of the Armenian troops, left at Lenkoran, terurned to Baku, as private individuals. These joined their Russian comrades in their disapproval of the British policy. To them, the paying off of old scores under the guise of punishment of the Tartars was more important than the quick establishment of peaceful conditions, which was our desire. The refusal of the British to destroy the Tartar Government raised a storm which the establishment of a coalition government did not appease . . . [293]

The discord among the newly indepentent states in the Caucasus, primarily on territorial and border issues, gave rise to foreign threats. On April 25, 1919, delegates from Azerbaijan, Dagestan, Georgia, and Armenia gathered in Tiflis to hold the Caucasian Conference. Convened to deal with political, economic, financial, and border issues of the region, the conference revealed sharp differences among the participating countries on territorial and border questions. However, the offensive of the former czarist general Denikin's voluntary army on Dagestan made the delegates abandon the conference unfinished.

With the intention of restoring the borders of "one and undivided Russia," Denikin intruded the territory of the North Caucasus Mountaineers Republic in spring 1919 and captured Derbent. It was clear that the czarist general had planned aggression against Azerbaijan. An extraordinary session of the parliament on June 11, 1919, resolved to establish a State Defense Committee, which assumed the entire governing authority.

Georgia, alarmed with the threat from Denikin's army as well, signed a mutual defense pact with Azerbaijan. The pact

---

[293] Excerpts from the report of the 2nd British occupation of Baku by General D. I. Shuttleworth. The British Archives 6479639, WO 106/1562.

stipulated mutual military assistance between the two countries in case of any foreign encroachment on their sovereignty and territory. The military agreement was signed for three years and allowed for Armenia to join it within two weeks. But Armenia preferred to sign a secret covenant with Denikin. The Azerbaijani-Georgian military pact provided for supply of 12 small cannons, 12 mountain cannons, 24 machine guns, 3,000 five-charge rifles, 211 sabers, 795 lances, and other arms from Georgia to Azerbaijan.[294]

4.8. The Azerbaijani Delegation at the Paris Peace Conference

Despite the end of World War I in November 1918, it took a while to finalize its consequences. The winners concurred to call an international peace conference in Paris to settle the major postwar issues in the world.

The parliament of Azerbaijan concluded to delegate a plenipotentiary mission with large discretion to the peace conference. The parliament's chairman, Topchubashov, was appointed to lead the mission. The main purpose of sending an Azerbaijani delegation to the peace conference was to gain international recognition of the Azerbaijani Democratic Republic. Acceptance of Azerbaijan's independence by neighboring countries did not fully alleviate the fragility of the new state. Only

---

[294] *Azerbaijanskaia Demokraticheskaia Respublika (1918-1920). Armiia (dokumenty i materaly)* [The Azerbaijani Democratic Republic (1918-1920). The Army (Documents and records)] (Baku, 1998), pp. 108-109.

ANAR ISGENDERLI

recognition by the Great Powers could help rebuff the aggression of Denikin's army and Soviet Russia.

Prior to the opening of the Paris Peace Conference, Topchubashov spearheaded extensive preparatory work in Istanbul, met with the Ottoman government members, Ukrainian, Russian, Persian, United States, Italian, Swedish, Dutch, and Armenian officials, exchanged views on the international situation and the purposes pursued at the peace conference, and informed them of the situation in Azerbaijan. The meetings with the Persian and the Russian envoys were the most important in regard to the issue of maintaining the independence of Azerbaijan.

Propagators of the anti-Azerbaijani campaign undertaken by Armenians in Europe and the United States denied existence of an independent state of Azerbaijan and by all means provided biased information to the leaders of the Allied Powers. The French government, influenced by Armenians and White Russians, made various excuses to keep the Azerbaijani delegation out of the conference and delayed the arrival of the mission for three months.

Having started its work in January 1919, the Paris Peace Conference dispatched a mission to Russia's former south provinces to survey the social, political, and economic situation from the ground. The mission included thirty delegates; most of them were Americans. The Commission on the Caucasus was led by Benjamin Moore, who asked the following questions from Topchubashov and Hajinski:

1. Could Azerbaijan exist as a politically and economically independent country?

2. Do you have sufficient material and moral strength for independence?
3. Could a federation or a confederation be established in the Caucasus or Transcaucasia?
4. If a Russian Federative Republic is created, would Azerbaijan consider joining this federation?
5. Do you assume a possibility of being taken under auspices of any other country?[295]

The Azerbaijani delegates answered in the affirmative to the first two questions but expressed doubts in regard to the issue of establishment of a federation. Topchubashov wrote, "The Allies are inclined to compromise with the stiff Armenian demands. Willing to create Great Armenia on the account of Turkey and Azerbaijan, the Armenians refused to join our federation."[296] In response to the fifth question, Topchubashov expressed a desire to gain support of the United States under the Wilsonian principles since this country did not have any economic interest in Azerbaijan.

Having waited for permission to join the conference since January 1919, the Azerbaijani mission finally arrived in Paris in early May, with the British's help, after three months of intense diplomatic and political struggle. On May 28, 1919, the Azerbaijani delegates were received by U.S. President Wilson. In a memo handed to President Wilson, the delegation described the history of establishment of the republic in Azerbaijan and sacrifices

---

[295] A. Topchubashov, *Paris məktubları* [Letters from Paris] (Baku, 1998), p. 24.
[296] Ibid., pp. 24-25.

ANAR ISGENDERLI

made on the path to freedom. The memo noted that throughout this struggle, 2 Azerbaijani towns and over 500 villages had been destroyed, and roughly 150,000 Muslim civilians had perished. In the Erivan *guberniya* alone 200 Muslim villages had been put on fire, and 200,000 Muslims had lost shelter in a very short time.[297] The delegation requested the president to recognize the independence of Azerbaijan, apply the Wilsonian principles of self-determination[298] to Azerbaijan, admit Azerbaijan to the League of Nations, render the U.S. military assistance to Azerbaijan, and aid the Azerbaijani delegation in establishment of diplomatic and economic relationships between Azerbaijan and the United States.[299] However, Woodrow Wilson suggested to the Azerbaijani delegation to support the idea of confederation and accept one of the Great Powers' auspice over the confederation under a mandate from the League of Nations. The Azerbaijani and, partially, the Georgian missions positively viewed the establishment of a confederation. The Armenian mission endeavored to undermine the plans. The Armenians called upon the conference presidium

---

[297] SARA, col. 894, list 10, file 94, sheets 66-67.

[298] The principles read, (1) A nation should be distinguished by its intellectual, moral and religious features; (2) A nation should prove its capability to decide its own fate; (3) It should possess economic, natural and financial resources to cover its expenditures; (4) It should be capable of defending against foreign aggression; (5) It must have suffered from oppression of the parent state.

[299] A. Raevskii, *Musavatskoe pravitel'stvo na Versal'skoi konferentsii. Donesenia predsedatelia azerbaijanskoi musavatskoi delaqatsii* [The Musavat Government at the Paris Conference. Speeches of the Chairman of the Azerbaijani Musavat Delegation] (Baku, 1931), pp. 39-40.

to take cognizance of the Armenian contribution to the Entente's victory and requested the Great Powers to facilitate in the creation of Great Armenia. The Armenians claimed a vast territory, including seven eastern provinces of Turkey, the Erivan *guberniya*, the southern parts of the Tiflis and the Elizavetpol (Ganja) *guberniyas*, and the territories of Kars and Ardahan. Besides, they also counted on a war indemnity in the amount of nineteen billion francs.[300]

On the other side, the Persian envoys to the Paris Peace Conference submitted a memo by which they demanded annexation of Baku, Derbent, Shaki, Shamakhi, Ganja, Karabakh, Nakhchivan, and Erivan. Persia, which had been an outsider in the war, was unsurprisingly denied the claims. Moreover, the Persian mission was sent off immediately after signing a treaty with Great Britain on August 9, 1919. On March 21, 1920, Persia declared recognition of Azerbaijan as an independent state and concluded a treaty of friendship with Azerbaijan.[301]

Eventually, on January 11, 1920, the Supreme Council of the Paris Peace Conference unanimously resolved to recognize *de facto* the independence of Azerbaijan. The news reached Azerbaijan on January 14 and was jubilantly received in the parliament. The foreign envoys attending the session joined the members of the parliament in commemorating their compatriots and the Ottoman soldiers who sacrificed their lives in the cause of independence. On this occasion, the Parliament announced a general amnesty on February 9, 1920.[302] Over

---

[300] *Azerbaijan* newspaper (May 18, 1919).

[301] SARA, col. 970, list 1, file 101, sheets 2-3.

[302] Mir Yakub, *Beynelmilel siyasetde petrol* [Oil in international politics] (Istanbul, 1928), p. 121.

three hundred Armenian criminals, proven to be guilty in 1918 massacres of Muslims in Baku, Shamakhi, Guba, and other *uyezds* of Azerbaijan, were set free.

On January 19, the Azerbaijani and the Georgian missions received an invitation to the Supreme Council of the Paris Peace Conference. The Allies formally assumed the obligation to defend the newly recognized states of the South Caucasus from foreign aggression. Apart from two hundred million *puds* of refined oil, Azerbaijan also was obliged to supply cotton, wool, silk, and animal skin in exchange for one hundred steam engines, two thousand tanks, and five hundred covered railroad cars to be delivered from Europe and the United States.[303]

4.9. The Government's Activity

Despite the lack of any previous experience in statecraft, the leadership of the Azerbaijani Democratic Republic managed to create a normally operating state machine, estabishing relations with more than twenty countries, including Turkey, Georgia, Armenia, Persia, Belgium, Holland, Greece, Denmark, Italy, France, Switzerland, the United Kingdom, the United States, Ukraine, Lithuania, Poland, and Finland on consulate-general and consular agency levels.[304]

---

[303] Ibid., p. 129.
[304] *Azerbaijanskaia Demokraticheskaia Respublika (1918-1920). Vneshnaia politika (doku¬menti i materiali)* [The Azerbaijani Democratic Republic (1918-20). Foreign policy (Documents and records)] (Baku, 1998), p. 196.

In form, Azerbaijan was a parliamentary republic. During the period of functioning in Ganja, on June 27, 1918, the cabinet declared the Azerbaijani language the official state language of the Azerbaijani Republic. Due to insufficiency of educated personnel with fluent Azerbaijani, the government temporarily permitted to use the Russian language in public offices. On June 24, the government adopted a national flag with white crescent and eight-point star on the red background, eventually replaced by a three-strip (green, red, and blue) background on November 9. On June 26, the government enacted the establishment of a Detached Army of Azerbaijan. Later, on August 11, it declared a general mobilization and called in all Azerbaijani citizens born between 1894 and 1899. It stipulated the establishment of a War Ministry on November 1. A month later, on December 25, the government undertook major military appointments: Samedaga Mehmandarov was appointed the Minister of War, General Aliaga Shykhlinski became his deputy, and General Suleyman Sulkevich assumed the position of the Chief of Staff. The military budget reached four hundred million manats in 1919. The process of army buildup was principally completed by January 1920 to include thirty thousand of infantry and ten thousand of cavalry troops.[305]

On August 23, 1918, the government adopted Regulations of Azerbaijani Citizenship. Another important step was the establishment of the Extraordinary Investigation Commission on July 15 to scrutinize the acts of genocide of the Azerbaijani population by Dashnak Armenian gangs. Establishment of

---

[305] Ibid., p. 104

ANAR ISGENDERLI

the Parliament (December 7, 1918), adoption of official state symbols (June 21, 1918), and recognition of equality of men and women were among the major achievements of the new republic. Azerbaijan also confirmed the separation of powers among legislative, executive, and judicial authorities.

In January and February 1919, the government established governorates in Karabakh and Nakhchivan, respectively, to put an end to Armenian atrocities and defend civilians from armed Armenian detachments.

On July 21, 1919, the Parliament enacted the Statute on Elections to the Constituent Assembly of the Republic of Azerbaijan.[306] A few weeks later, on August 11, the Parliament passed another important law on Azerbaijani Citizenship, which recognized former Russian nationals whose parents or themselves were born on the territory of Azerbaijan as citizens of Azerbaijan regardless of their ethnic or religious identity.

Public education was among primary concerns of the government. Roughly half of the schools switched to use the Azerbaijani language, which became a compulsory subject. Another essential step was establishment of the Baku University on September 1, 1919. A number of boys' and girls' secondary schools were opened in the provinces of the country, and up to one hundred young men received government scholarships to study in European universities. Establishment of the Azerbaijani Chamber of Appeals, Intelligence and Counter-Intelligence Departments, and the Organization for

---

[306] *Azərbaycan Xalq Cümhuriyyəti (1918-1920). Parlament* [The People's Republic of Azerbaijan (1918-1920). Parliament] volume 1 (Baku, 1998), p. 876.

Combatting Counter-Revolution became the vital pillar of the state-building process. The Baku-Batum oil pipeline was restored in 1919 to provide monetary influx into the country. To revitalize the domestic commerce, the government issued a decree on free trade (August 27, 1918) and gave rebirth to the merchant fleet (October 30, 1918). The Caspian Fleet of Azerbaijan was established in summer 1919.

The territory of the Azerbaijani Democratic Republic was 97,300 square kilometers (or roughly 37,600 square miles). 8,700 square kilometers (3,360 square miles) on the border with Georgia and 7,900 square kilometers (3,000 square miles) on the border with Armenia were considered by the Government of Azerbaijan as contested areas. The population of Azerbaijan was 2,862,000 people; 70 percent of them were Muslims.[307]

During the twenty-three months of independence, the Azerbaijani Democratic Republic was governed by five subsequent cabinets, with first three chaired by Fatali Khan Khoyski and the other two led by Nasib Yusifbeyli.

Within seventeen months of functioning, the Azerbaijani Parliament, composed of 15 parties, held 145 sessions and passed some 230 acts to secure the interests of the entire nation.

4.10. Invasion by Soviet Russia

Despite international recognition of Azerbaijan, its northern borders continued to stay under threat. In a note sent to the Azerbaijani government, Chicherin, the commissar

---

[307] *Almanac of Azerbaijan Republic* (Baku, 1920), p. 93.

on Foreign Affair of Soviet Russia, proposed a military alliance with Azerbaijan to jointly oppose Denikin's army. It was evident for the Azerbaijani leadership that the Soviet government was attempting to involve and exhaust the young state in an unequal military conflict with Denikin and consequently deprive it of its independence. Azerbaijan's foreign minister Khoyski replied that the struggle of the Soviet government against Denikin was an internal affair of the Russian people, and the government of Azerbaijan had no intention to interfere in domestic issues of Russia. Chicherin's second note dated January 23 failed to recognize the independence of Azerbaijan and accused the Azerbaijani government of refusal to fight against Denikin's troops. In return, Khoyski demanded unconditional recognition of Azerbaijan's sovereignty by Soviet Russia. Chicherin's next note of March 7 was nothing but trickery and procrastination. Over time, it was becoming clear that these games were aimed at masking military preparations for invasion of Azerbaijan and reduce vigilance of the Azerbaijani government. The genuine attitude of Soviet Russia toward Azerbaijan was perfectly reflected in Lenin's telegram to the members of the Military-Revolutionary Council of the Caucasus Front, Smilga and Orjonikidze, sent on March 17, 1920: "It is very critical to capture Baku. Concentrate all your efforts on this."[308]

---

[308] *Internatsional'naia pomosh XI Armii v bor'be za pobedu sovetskoi vlasti v Azerbaijane. Dokumenti i materialı. 1920-1921 gg.* [International aid to the 11th army in the fight for the victory of the Soviet power in Azerbaijan. Documents and records. 1920-1921] (Baku, 1989), p. 17.

The government's tardiness to introduce land reforms was cleverly employed by the Bolsheviks. In early 1919, they provoked uprisings among peasants in a number of *uyezds*, with the fiercest insurrection organized in Ganja. The uprising was suppressed by September 1919.[309]

On February 11-12, 1920, the Bolsheviks founded the Communist Party of Azerbaijan in Baku. The actual leader of the Bolshevik party was Anastas Mikoyan, an inveterate enemy of the Azerbaijani nation. The party's objective was to overthrow the incumbent government and establish a Soviet rule in Azerbaijan through an armed revolt.[310]

In parallel, Soviet Russia also exploited Armenia's enmity toward Azerbaijan. In early 1920, Armenian envoys in Moscow, Priumov, and Zaharian offered assistance in overthrowing the government in Azerbaijan in exchange for territorial concessions. The Armenian proposal included insurgencies among the Armenian population of Karabakh and Ganjabasar and a war to be launched by Armenia against Azerbaijan. In March 1920, in the days of Novruz festivities, almost all Azerbaijani troops were engaged in suppression of Armenian riots in Karabakh, leaving the northern borders undefended. Meantime, 72,000 Russian troops were approaching the Azerbaijani border near the river Samur. The aid promised to the Azerbaijani government from the West had not appeared.

---

[309] E. A. Tokarzhevskii, *Iz istorii inostrannoi interventsii i qrazhdanskoi voiny v Azerbaijane* [Glimpses of history of the foreign intervention and the civil war in Azerbaijan] (Baku, 1957), p. 249.

[310] *Azərbaycan Kommunist Partiyası tarixinin oçerkləri* [Essays on the history of the Communist Party of Azerbaijan] (Baku, 1986), p. 199.

Members of the Azerbaijani Cabinet did not share a common view on how to deal with Soviet Russia: Foreign Minister Khoyski was a hard-liner, while Minister of Interrior Mammad Hasan Hajinski was inclined to negotiate and make terms with local Bolsheviks. Hajinski argued that by making considerable concessions to Russia, Azerbaijan could preserve its independence.

In the meeting of the cabinet in March 1920, Hajinski gained a solid support from his adherents; in the circumstances, Prime Minister Yusifbeyli had to resign. Hajinski was assigned to form a new cabinet. However, he procrastinated and shortly joined the Bolshevik party himself.

The British archives contain an interesting description of Nasib Bey Yusifbeyli. In a letter to headquarters in London, the British high commissioner in the Caucasus, Wardrop, writes, "Prime Minister Yusifbeyli is an accurate, well-educated, sharp-witted, liberal, sincere, faithful, outcome driven and gracious man. The long delay by the Allies to determine Azerbaijan's political status hampers his work. Prime Minister's ideas are rather nationalistic than religious. He detests Bolshevism . . . His only desire is to see his country independent . . . His team and cabinet could be a role model for some European countries. The people and the government of this country have much better attitude toward Great Britain than in any other country. If we help them, they will faithfully collaborate with the United Kingdom."[311]

---

[311] *Azərbaycan Xalq Cümhuriyyəti. Böyük Britaniyanın arxiv sənədləri* [The People's Republic of Azerbaijan. Archive records of Great Britain] (Baku, 2008), p. 18.

The delay in forming of a new cabinet exacerbated the situation. The strife among the parliamentary factions reached its peak. Leadership of the Ittihad Party, which was in a continuing opposition to the incumbent authority and striving to overthrow it, demanded conclusion of military alliance with Russia. Azerbaijani Bolsheviks called for an appeal to the Russian government for military aid and clamored to bring in Russia's Eleventh Army under the veil of establishing law and order in the country.

In April 1920, after defeating Denikin's troops, the Eleventh Red Army approached the border of Azerbaijan. On April 15, Khoyski sent a note to Chicherin demanding explanations of the reasons and purpose of the Russian troop's concentration on the border with Azerbaijan. However, the note was ignored by Chicherin. In the meantime, the Communist (Bolshevik) Party of Azerbaijan sent a delegation to the town of Petrovsk to discuss the details of a Russian intervention in Azerbaijan. On behalf of the people of Azerbaijan, the local Bolsheviks, led by Mikoyan, invited the Russian army into Azerbaijan. The jointly elaborated plan envisaged an armed revolt twenty-four hours prior to entering of the Eleventh Russian Army into the territory of Azerbaijan. The plan sought to convince the international community that the Azerbaijani government fell in consequence of an internal revolt rather than the foreign military intervention. However, Russia's Eleventh Army did not wait for a rebellion to start in Baku, crossed the frontier on the night of April 26, and moved toward Baku. The insignificant number of border guard troops was helpless to resist the invaders. The deputy minister of war, Shikhlinski, had countermanded orders for the explosion of railroad bridges. The "auxiliary regiment" guarding the vital sites in the city, including the building of the parliament, defected to the Bolsheviks. Guns on the warships in the Baku bay were aimed at the Parliament building.

Simultaneously with the invasion of the Russian army, the Central Committee of the Communist (Bolsheviks') Party of Azerbaijan, in conjunction with the Baku Bureau of the Caucasus Regional Committee of the Russian Communist (Bolsheviks') Party, presented a surrender ultimatum to the Parliament. The ultimatum was discussed in the last meeting of the Parliament on April 27 under the chairmanship of M. Y. Jafarov. The meeting lasted three hours (from 08:45 p.m. to 11:45 p.m.). At the suggestion of Rasulzade, the doors remained open for the public during deliberations. Hajinski informed the Parliament members of the ultimatum, which demanded surrender of all authorities to the Communists the same evening; otherwise, the Central Committee of the Azerbaijani Communists threatened to make every effort to surrender power to the Red Army. The Communists also warned that a failure to surrender the same night would lead to a ban of political parties, including the Musavat. Hajinski also related that the Communists had refused to consider any of the government's proposals and had notified that in case of repudiation of voluntary surrender, the entire responsibility for consequences would be born by the members of the Parliament. In conclusion, Hajinski called the parliamentarians to make the only right decision "for the sake of saving the nation." Many of the Parliament members made a stand against unconditional surrender of power to the Communists. At the same time, they declared that the authority could be surrendered to the

Communists under certain conditions, the foremost of them being independence of the country. Eventually, the majority in the Parliament voted for passing the authorities to the Communists of Azerbaijan under the below conditions:

1. The Russian army shall not enter Baku but transit by rail to aid Anatolia.[312]
2. The independence and the territory of Azerbaijan shall be protected from any kind of aggression and annexation.
3. The Army of Azerbaijan shall remain as is.
4. The political parties of Azerbaijan shall enjoy freedom of activity.
5. Former statesmen, members of the Parliament and the Cabinet shall not be persecuted, public servants shall maintain their jobs, and only executive officials shall be superseded.
6. Azerbaijani Councils shall confer freely to determine the form of government.

---

[312] The Ottoman Empire was defeated in World War I and faced a threat of being splitted among the winners. On the other hand, Russia, disengaged from the world war with the cumbrous Brest-Litovsk Peace Treaty, was stricken with civil war. A common attitute toward Western powers shared by Lenin's Soviet government and the Turkish forces led by Mustafa Kemal (Ataturk) brought these two camps together. The Soviet command utilized this factor and deceived both the local population and the international community by announcing that the main reason of transgressing the borders of Azerbaijan was sending troops in support of Ataturk's army through Azerbaijan's territory.

On April 29, the Revolutionary Committee of Azerbaijan appealed to Soviet Russia for military aid although the Russian army had entered the territory of Azerbaijan two days earlier. This marked the end of the twenty-three-month-long existence of the Azerbaijani Democratic Republic.

On April 28, 1920, the Bolsheviks proclaimed the establishment of the Soviet Socialist Republic of Azerbaijan. After taking over the power, the Bolsheviks did not adhere to the surrender conditions. Baku again lived through a week of looting; in parallel, the Red Army continued encroachment on Azerbaijani towns and villages. Thus, Russia's military intervention, flagrant violation of international law, and bloodshed by the Red Army resulted in the fall of the Azerbaijani Democratic Republic, recognized as an independent state by the Supreme Council of the Paris Peace Conference. The resistance movement of the Azerbaijani people in support of freedom and independent statehood was squashed; all government institutions of the Azerbaijani Republic were abolished. North Azerbaijan was reannexed by the Russian empire, this time under the guise of Bolshevism. The Azerbaijani nation was compelled to live under occupation until October 1991.

CONCLUSION

T HE SOUTH CAUCASUS is still embroiling. The forces that disturb stability and their patrons are known. It is also not a secret on who seized the other's territory by force and arms and expelled one million people. But it is not clear what goals are pursued by this expansionist policy. Today, when the world struggles against terror, there is a great need for all peace-defending nations to unite in this fight. In the words of late Austrian historian Erich Feigl, "Would I dare to write about these realities, if my friend was not killed by an Armenian terrorist?" The answer is yes. Erich Feigl cleared up the relationships between Turks and Armenians, disregarding ethnic and religious differences. May his soul find heavenly peace for the unbiased position he held in his books.

An American historian, Firuz Kazemzadeh, who had never been to the South Caucasus personally, carried notable researches on the region. Kazemzadeh emphasized that the Soviet regime deprived the Azerbaijani nation of everything and particularly of its history. Meanwhile, Armenians dispersed around the globe launched large-scale propaganda campaigns to convince the international community that they had allegedly been pursued and driven out of their historical homeland. Armenians claim without scruple that Turks are their enemies and continue to believe in this absurdity.

Another American researcher, Tadeusz Swietochowski, wrote that when Armenian nationalists established terrorist groups like the Hunchak and the Dashnaktsutiun in late nineteenth century, it was clear who they planned to fight against and where their support would come from. These organizations made no secret of what means they would utilize to achieve their goals. As to Muslims (Azerbaijanis), they confined themselves to establishment of only one organization, the Hummat, in early twentieth century. The goal of the group was more like a desire: to achieve solidarity of all Muslims of the world. However, this did not imply that other nations would be menaced or there were any views on their territories.

A Russian historian, Vasili Velichko, wrote that the annals of the Armenian history are full of controversies and grand names unknown to any historian; now and then people of dubious descent are described in superlatives. Armenia, a country with erratic borders, was under continuing vassalage of neighboring rulers, constantly betrayed by its questionable kings.

Ilia Chavchavadze, the prominent Georgian publicist of the nineteenth century, wrote on Armenians: "May all-mighty God bestow strength and ability to unite on them. Nevertheless, may they never defraud anyone; may they never abase us, and aggrandize and glorify themselves. We offered you shelter and harbored you, we fraternized with you. Do not treat us in our home like enemies. A lion on your way is better than a foe in your house."

One of the founding fathers of the Azerbaijani Democratic Republic, Alimerdan Bey Topchubashov, wrote from the Paris Peace Conference: "The Georgians are in sympathy with us on all issues connected with the future of the Caucasus. But the

Armenians nearly question our coexistence in the Caucasus by estranging from us and the Georgians. The Armenians forgot that we are here to achieve peace."

The twentieth century witnessed numerous tragedies in various countries of the world. The genocide of Azerbaijani civilians by the Armenian military in the town of Khojaly in February 1992 is remembered as one of the most violent atrocities of the century. The Armenian troops killed 613 innocent people overnight, mostly elderly, women, and children; 1,275 civilians were taken prisoners.

The Armenian military aggression on the Azerbaijani lands did not halt at the Khojaly tragedy. In 1992-93, Armenian armed forces laid hands on a number of native provinces of Azerbaijan, including Shusha, Lachin, Kalbajar, Agdam, Fizuli, Jabrayil, Qubadli, and Zangilan.

Azerbaijan has been negotiating for almost twenty years to return the captured territories. The four UN resolutions demanding immediate withdrawal of Armenian troops from the territory of Azerbaijan remain unfulfilled.

Notwithstanding these facts, today, Azerbaijan conducts an independent foreign policy, continues development, and ranks among the global leaders for the pace of economic growth. Azerbaijanis are a nation of peace-defending, tolerant, and hospitable people who wish for peaceful coexistence with their neighbors. At the same time, they wish for restoration of the historical territory of Azerbaijan, liberation of invaded lands, return of hundreds of thousands of refugees and forced internal migrants to their homes, recognition of the true facts by the international community, and identification and fair prosecution of the aggressor. May justice triumph!

The map of the South Caucasus officially submitted to the
Paris Peace Conference (1919)

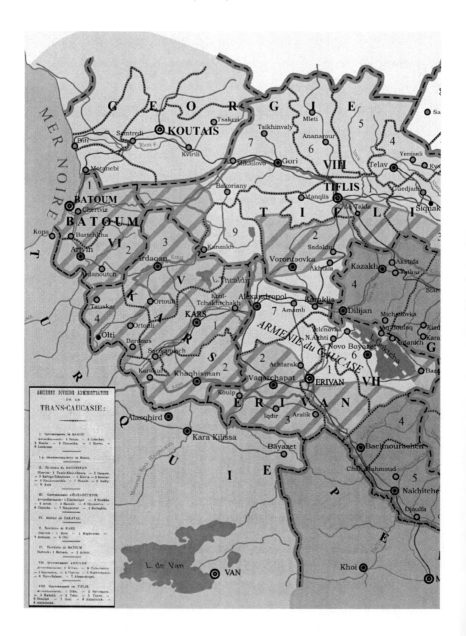

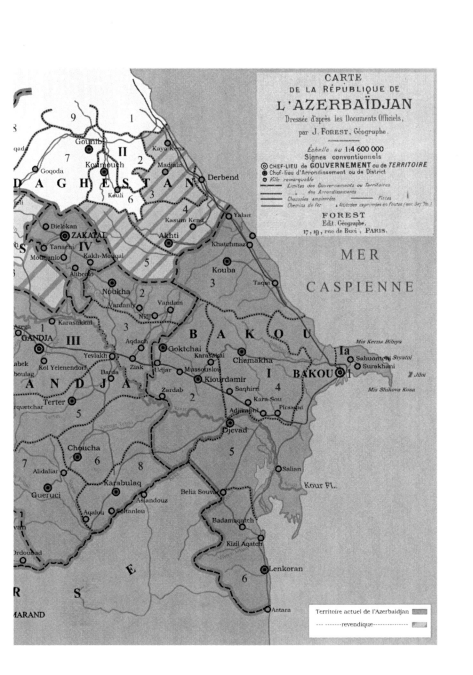

CARTE
DE LA RÉPUBLIQUE DE
L'AZERBAÏDJAN
Dressée d'après les Documents Officiels,
par J. FOREST, Géographe.

Échelle au 1:4 600 000
Signes conventionnels
CHEF-LIEU de GOUVERNEMENT ou de TERRITOIRE
Chef-lieu d'Arrondissement ou de District
Ville remarquable
Limites des Gouvernements ou Territoires
" des Arrondissements
Chaussées empierrées   Pistes
Chemins de fer   Militaires exprimées en Toutes (env. 3m⁷ /m.)
FOREST
Édit. Géographe,
17, 19, rue de Buci, PARIS.

MER

CASPIENNE

Territoire actuel de l'Azerbaïdjan
-----------revendique-----------

The building and the editorial office of Kaspii
newspaper burned and destroyed during the
March events of 1918.

Corpses of Azerbaijani victims of the March massacre
in Baku (1918).

Burned shops on Bazaar street in Baku (March, 1918).

Persian postcard devoted to the March 1918 massacre
in Baku. The title in Farsi reads, "The massacre of
Muslims in Baku and Iranian consul
witnessing the events."

Excavation of a mass grave of 1918 genocide
in Guba, Azerbaijan.

GLOSSARY

Akhund A Muslim cleric, common in Iran and Azerbaijan, responsible for leading religious services in a community.

Guberniya A major administrative subdivision of Imperial Russia.

Imam An Islamic leadership position, often the leader of a mosque and the community. Similar to spiritual leaders, the imam is the one who leads the prayer during Islamic gatherings.

Medrese or Madrasah A religious school in Azerbaijan and other Muslim countries.

Okrug A type of administrative division of oblasts and several guberniyas in Imperial Russia.

Pasha A high rank in the Ottoman Empire political system, typically granted to governors, generals and dignitaries. As an honorary title, *Pasha,* in one of its various ranks, is equivalent to the British title of *Lord.*

Pud An obsolete unit of mass equal to approximately 16.38 kilograms (36.11 pounds).

SAPPPMRA State Archive on Political Parties and Public Movements of the Republic of Azerbaijan.

SARA State Archives of the Republic of Azerbaijan.

The Transcaucasian Seim (*Sejm* or Polish for "assembly") The first government of the independent Transcaucasia established at Tbilisi in November 1917.

Uyezd An administrative subdivision of *guberniya* in Imperial Russia.

Verst(a) An obsolete Russian unit of length equal to 3,500 feet (1.0668 kilometers, or 0.6629 miles).

LIST OF REFERENCES

In the Azerbaijani Language

1. The State Archives of the Republic of Azerbaijan, collections: 100, 879, 894, 895, 970, 1061.

2. The State Archive on Political Parties and Public Movements of the Republic of Azerbaijan, collection 277.

3. *Azərbaycan Xalq Cümhuriyyətinin Ensiklopediyası [Encyclopedia of the People's Republic of Azerbaijan]*, in 2 volumes. Volume 1, Baku, 2004; Volume 2, Baku, 2005.

4. *Azərbaycan Xalq Cümhuriyyəti. Böyük Britaniyanın arxiv sənədləri [The People's Republic of Azerbaijan. Archive Records of Great Britain]*, Baku, 2008.

5. *Azərbaycan Xalq Cümhuriyyəti (1918-1920). Parlament [The People's Republic of Azerbaijan, 1918-20. Parliament]*, Volumes 1 and 2, Baku, 1998.

6. *Azərbaycan Kommunist Partiyası tarixinin oçerkləri [Essays on the History of the Communist Party of Azerbaijan]*, Baku, 1986.

7. *Azərbaycanda sosialist inqilabının qələbəsi uğrunda bolşeviklərin mübarizəsi. Sənədlər və materiallar. 1917-1918 [Bolsheviks' Struggle for the Victory of Socialist Revolution in Azerbaijan. Documents and Records. 1917-18]*, Baku, 1960.

8. I. Chavchavadze, *Erməni alimləri və fəryad edən daşlar [Armenian Savants and Outcrying Stones]*, Baku, 1995.

9. *Erməni terror və quldur birləşmələrinin bəşəriyyətə qarşı cinayətləri (XIX-XX əsrlər)* [*Crimes of the Armenian Terrorist Gangs against Humanity (19ᵗʰ-20ᵗʰ centuries)*], Baku, 2003.

10. J. Hasanov, *Azərbaycan beynəlxalq münasibətlər sistemində, 1918-1920* [*Azerbaijan as an Actor in the System of International Relations, 1918-20*], Baku, 1993.

11. A. Iskenderov, *Azərbaycanda türk-müsəlman soyqırımı probleminin tarixşünaslığı (1918-1920)* [*The Historiography of the Turk-Muslim Genocide in Azerbaijan*], Baku, 2006.

12. The *Kaspii* newspaper, April 16, 1917, issue 84.

13. M. Mammadzade, *Ermənilər və İran* [*Armenians and Persia*], Istanbul, 1927; reprinted: Baku, 1993.

14. M. Mammadzade, *Milli Azərbaycan hərəkatı* [*The Azerbaijani National Movement*], Berlin, 1938; reprinted: Baku, 1992.

15. M. Muradzade, *Mart hadise-i əliməsi* [*The March Events*], Baku, 1919; reprinted in 1996.

16. I. Mammadov, *Tariximiz, torpağımız, taleyimiz* [*Our History, Land, and Fate*], Baku, 2003.

17. Muhammad Asad Bey, *Şərqdə neft və qan* [*Oil and Blood in the East*], Baku, 2005.

18. M. S. Ordubadi, *Qanlı illər* [*The Bloody Years*], Baku, 1991.

19. S. Onullahi, *Erməni millətçiləri və İran* [*Armenian Nationalists and Persia*], Baku, 2002.

20. A. Pashayev, *Açılmamış səhifələrin izi ilə* [*The Trails of Unopened Pages*], Baku, 2001.

21. S. J. Pishavari, *Seçilmiş əsərləri* [*Selected Works*], Baku, 1965.

22. S. Sardariniya, *Arazın hər iki tayında müsəlmanların soyqırımı* [*The Muslim Genocide on Both Sides of Aras*], Baku, 2006.

23. A. Topchubashov, *Paris məktubları* [*Letters from Paris*], Baku, 1998.

24. *Zaqafqaziya Seyminin Müsəlman fraksiyası və Azərbaycan Milli Şurası iclaslarının protokolları* [*Minutes of Meetings of the Muslim Faction of Transcaucasian Seim and the Azerbaijani National Council*], Baku, 2006.

25. A. Ziyadxanlı, *Azərbaycan*, Baku, 1919; reprinted: Baku, 1993.

In the Turkish Language

26. *Azerbaycan* journal, 1993, July-October.

27. *Azerbaycan* journal, 1962, issue no. 7.

28. *Azerbaycan belgelerinde ermeni sorunu (1918-1920)* [*The Armenian Question in the Provinces of Azerbaijan (1918-20)*], Ankara, 2001.

29. H. Baykara, *Azerbaycan istiklal mücadelesi tarihi* [*History of the Struggle for Independence of Azerbaijan*], Istanbul, 1975; reprinted: Baku, 1992.

30. Erdaş Nilgün. *Milli mücadile döneminde Kafkas Cümhuriyyetleri ilə ilişkiler (1917-1921)* [*Relationships with the Republics of Caucausus at the time of the National Struggle (1917-21)*], Ankara, 1994.

31. *Kut'ül Amare Kahramanı Halil Paşa'nın Anıları: Bitmeyen Savaş* [*Halil Pasha, the Hero of Kut-al-Amara: an Unfinished War*], Istanbul, 1972.

32. Kazım Karabekir, *Erzincan ve Erzurum kurtuluşu* [*The Liberation of Erzinjan and Erzurum*], Ankara, 1990.

33. *İngilizlerin Mavi Kitap'ına Sovyetler'in Yanıtı Kızıl Kitap Güneybatı Kafkas'ta Taşnak Mezalimi* (translated by Kayhan Yükseler) [*The Red Book of the Soviets in reply to the Blue Guide of England: Dashnak Atrocities in the Southwestern Caucasus*], Istanbul, 2006.

34. Karibi, *Ermeni iddialarına yanıt gürcü devletinin kırmızı kitapı* [*The Red Book of the Georgian Government in reply to the Armenian Claims*], Istanbul, 2007.

35. N. Keykurun, *Azerbaycan istiklalı mücadelesi hatiraları* [*Memoirs of the Struggle for Independence in Azerbaijan*], Istanbul, 1964.

36. A. N. Kurat, *Türkiye və Rusya* [*Turkey and Russia*], Ankara, 1990.

37. Mir Yakub, *Beynelmilel siyasetde petrol* [*Oil in the International Politics*], Istanbul, 1928.

38. Onk Nizamettin, "Yeni Azerbaycan kurularken" ["While Building New Azerbaijan"], *Türk Dünyası* journal of history, April 1992.

39. M. Saray, *Azerbaycan türkleri tarihi* [*History of Azerbaijani Turks*], Istanbul, 1993.

40. Süleyman İzzet, *15 piyade tümeninin Azerbaycan və Şimali Kafkasiyadakı harekati və müharibeleri* [*15th Infantry Division's Movements and Battles in Azerbaijan and the North Caucasus in WWI*], Ankara, 1936.

41. Süleyman Kocabaş, *Ermeni sorunu nedir ve ne değildir* [*What Is and What Is Not the Armenian Question*], Istanbul, 1958.

42. T. Sünbül, *Azerbaycan dosyası* [*The Azerbaijani File*], Ankara, 1980.

43. Türk Silahlı Kuvvetleri Askeri Tarih ve Strateji Etüt Başkanlığı arşivi (ATASE) [The Archive of the Turkish General Staff Military History and Strategic Research and Inspection Directorate], col. 1, col. 3820, col. 5309.

44. Şahin Ergün, *Trabzon ve Batum konfransları ve anlaşmaları (1917-1918)* [*The Conferences and the Treaties of Trabzon and Batum (1917-18)*], Ankara, 2002.

45. E. Rüştü, *Büyük harpda Bakü yollarında* [*On the Way to Baku during the Great War*], Ankara, 1934.

46. N. Yucer, *Birinci dünya savaşında Osmanlı ordusunun Azerbaycan ve Dağıstan harekatı* [*The Campaigns of the Ottoman Army in Azerbaijan and Dagestan during World War I*], Ankara, 1996.

In the Russian Language

47. *'Armyanskiy genotsid': mif i realnost* [*'Armenian Genocide': Myth and Reality*], Baku, 1992.

48. The *Azerbaijan* newspaper, May 18, 1919.

49. Aktı, sobranniye Kavkazkoyu Arxeograficheskoyu Komissieyu (AKAK) [*Records compied by The Caucasus Archeographic Commission (RCAC)*], volume 7, Tiflis, 1878.

50. *Aktı, sobranniye Kavkazkoyu Arxeograficheskoyu Komissieyu (AKAK)* [*Records compied by The Caucasus Archeographic Commission (RCAC)*], volume 10, Tiflis, 1885.

51. T. Akopian, *İstoriia Yerevana* [*History of Yerevan*], Yerevan, 1975.

52. Ch. Agaian, *Rol' Rossii v istoricheskikh sud'bakh armianskogo naroda* [*Russia's Role in the Historic Foredoom of the Armenian People*], Moscow, 1978.

53. *Azerbaijanskaia Demokraticheskaia Respublika (1918-1920).* *Armiia (dokumenty i materaly)* [*The Azerbaijani Democratic Republic (1918-20). The Army (Documents and Records)*], Baku, 1998.

54. *Azerbaijanskaia Demokraticheskaia Respublika (1918-1920).* *Vneshniaia politika (dokumenty i materialy)* [*The Azerbaijani Democratic Republic (1918-20). Foreign Policy (Documents and Records)*], Baku, 1998.

55. B. Baikov, "Vospominaniya o revolutsii v Zakavkaz'e (1917-1920)" ["The Memories of the Revolution in Transcaucasia (1917-20)"], *Archive of the Russian Revolution*, volume 9, Berlin, 1922.

56. *Bol'sheviki v bor'be za pobedu sotsialisticheskoi revolutsii v Azerbaijane. Dokumenty i materialy. 1917-1918 gody* [*Bolsheviks in the Fight for the Victory of the Socialist Revolution in Azerbaijan. Documents and Records. 1917-18*], Baku, 1957.

57. *Garegin Nzhde i yeqo uchenie* [*The Teaching of Garegin Nzhdeh and Its Relevance*], Yerevan, 2004.

58. Herodotus. *Istoriia* [*History*], Leningrad, 1972.

59. S. Glinka, *Opisanie pereseleniia armian azerbaijanskikh v peredel Rossii* [*Description of the Ressetlement of Azerbaijani Armenians to the Territory of Russia*], Moscow, 1831; reprinted: Baku, 1990.

60. V. Grigoriev, *Statisticheskoie opisanie Nakhichevanskoi provintsii* [*Statistical Description of the Nakhchivan Province*], St. Petersburg, 1833.

61. *Grazhdanskoie upravlenie Zakavkaz'em ot prisoedineniia Gruzii do namestnichestva Velikogo Kniazia Mikhaila Nikolaevicha* [*Civil Governance in Transcaucasia from*

ANAR ISGENDERLI

Georgia's Accession to Viceroyalty of Grand Duke Mikhail Nikolayevich], Tiflis, 1901.

62. L. Dabagian, *Voprosy istorii* [*Questions of History*], Moscow, 1929.

63. N. Dubrovin, *Zakavkaz'ev 1803-1806 godakh* [*Transcaucasia in 1803-06*], St. Petersburg, 1866.

64. *Dokumenty i materialy po vneshnei politike Zakavkaz'ia i Gruzii* [*Documents and Records on the Foreign Policy of Transcaucasia and Georgia*], Tiflis, 1969.

65. Lionel Charles Dunsterville, *Britanskii imperializm v Baku i Persii v 1917-1918 g.* [*British Imperialism in Baku and Persia in 1917-18*], Tiflis, 1925.

66. M. M. Diakonov, *Predystoriia armianskogo naroda* [*Pre-History of the Armenian People*], Yerevan, 1968.

67. A. D. Eritsov, "Dannye ob armianskom naselenii v Rossii" ["Data on the Armenian Population in Russia"], published in *The Bulletin of the Caucasus Branch of the Imperial Russian Geographic Society*, volume 1, Tiflis, 1881.

68. Esai Hasan-Jalalian, *Kratkaia istoria strany Albanskoi (1702-1722 gg)* [*Brief History of the Country of Albania (1702-22)*], Baku, 1989.

69. B. Ishkhanian, *Narodnosti Kavkaza. (Statistiko-ekonomicheskoe issledovanie)* [*Ethnicities in The Caucasus. A Statistical-Economic Reseach*], St. Petersburg, 1916.

70. B. Ishkhanian, *Velikie uzhasy v qor. Baku. Anketnoe issledovanie sentiabrskikh sobıtii 1918 g.* [*Atrocities in the city of Baku. A Questionnaire Survey of September Events of 1918*], Tiflis, 1920.

71. *Istoriia XIX veka* [*The History of the 19ᵗʰ Century*], edited by professors Lavisse and Rambaud, Translated from French, volume 8, Moscow, 1939.

72. K. Imanov, *Armianskie inorodnyie skazki* [*Tall Armenian Tales*], Baku, 2008.

73. *Internatsional'naia pomosh XI Armii v bor'be za pobedu sovetskoi vlasti v Azerbaijane. Dokumentı i materialı. 1920-1921 gg.* [*International Aid to the 11ᵗʰ Army in the Fight for the Victory of the Soviet Power in Azerbaijan. Documents and Records. 1920-21*], Baku, 1989.

74. A. B. Kadishev, *Interventsiia i grazhdanskaia voina v Zakavkaz'e* [*The Intervention and the Civil War in the Transcaucasia*], Moscow, 1960.

75. *Kavkazskii kalendar' na 1855 g.* [*The Caucasus Almanac for the year of 1955*], Tiflis, 1855.

76. Y. D. Lazarev, *Prichiny bedstvii armian v Turtsii* [*The Reasons of Armenian Miseries in Turkey*], Tiflis, 1899.

77. J. Malevil, *Armianskaia tragedia 1915 goda* [*The Armenian Tragedy of 1915*], Baku, 1990.

78. R. Mustafaev, *Marshy Smerti. Prestuplenia armianstva protiv yevreiskogo naroda* [*The Marches of Death. Armenian Crimes against the Jewish Nation*], Baku, 2008.

79. I. Mamedov, *Trilogia panarmenizma. Kovarnaia strategia chereduiushikhsia agressii* [*The Trilogy of Pan-Armenism. The Insidious Strategy of Alternating Aggressions*], Baku, 2006.

80. *Materialy po izucheniu Nakhichevanskoi SSR* [*Study materials on the Nakhchivan SSR*], Tiflis, 1933.

81. S. S. Pastermasian, *Zapadnaia Armenia v kontse XIX v.* [*West Armenia in late 19ᵗʰ Century*], M., 1949.

82. *Polnoie sobranie zakonov Rossiiskoi imperii* [*Complete Collection of Laws of the Russian Empire*], Collection 2, volume 3, St. Petersburg, 1830.

83. V. A. Potto, *Kavkazskaya voyna. Persidskaya voyna 1826-1828 gg.* [*The Caucasian War. The Persian War in 1826-1828*], volume 3, Saint-Petersburg 1911; reprinted: Stavropol, 2005.

84. V. A. Parsamian, *Istoriia armianskogo naroda. 1801-1900 gg* [*History of the Armenian People. 1801-1900*], book 1, Yerevan, 1977.

85. *Pravitel'stvennyi vestnik* [*The Government Bulletin*], St. Petersburg, 1878.

86. *Prisoedinenie Vostochnoi Armenii k Rossii. Sbornik dokumentov* [*Accession of East Armenia to Russia. Collection of Documents*], volume 1, (1801-1813), Yerevan, 1972.

87. A. Raevskii, *Musavatskoe pravitel'stvo na Versal'skoi konferentsii. Donesenia predsedatelia azerbaijanskoi musavatskoi delaqatsii* [*The Musavat Government at the Versailles Conference. Speeches of the Chairman of the Azerbaijani Musavat Delegation*], Baku, 1931.

88. Saleh Bey. *Armianstvo* [*The Armenism*], Baku, 1994.

89. S. E. Sef, *Kak bol'sheviki prishli k vlasti v 1917-1918 gg. v Bakinskom raione* [*How Bolsheviks Came to Power in 1917-18 in Baku*], Baku, 1927.

90. Traktat mezhdu Karabakhskim khanom i Rossiiskoi imperiei o perekhode khanstva pod vlast' Rossii ot 14 maia 1805 goda [The Treaty between the Khan of Karabakh and the Russian Empire on Accession of the Khanate to Russia].

91. Tacitus Cornelius, *Sochinenia* [*Writings*], volume 2, St. Petersburg, 1887.

92. E. A. Tokarzhevskii, *Iz istorii inostrannoi interventsii i qrazhdanskoi voiny v Azerbaijane* [*Glimpses of History of the Foreign Intervention and the Civil War in Azerbaijan*], Baku, 1957.

93. N. N. Shavrov, *Novaia ugroza russkomu delu v Zakavkaz'e. Predstoiashaia rasprodazha Mugani inorodtsam* [*The New Threat to the Russian Cause in Transcaucasia. The Forthcoming Sale of Mughan to Aliens*], Baku, 1990.

94. Suren Shaumian, *Bakinskaia Kommuna* [*The Baku Commune*], Baku, 1927.

95. I. Shopen, *Istoricheskii pamiatnik sostoiania Armianskoi oblasti (Erivanskoi gubernii) v epokhu prisoedinenia k Rossiiskoi imperii* [*Historical Memorial of the Situation in the Armenian Oblast' (the Erivan guberniya) in the Days of Accession to the Russian Empire*], St. Petersburg, 1852.

96. V. L. Velichko, *Russkoe delo i mezhduplemennyie voprosy* [*The Russian Cause and the Inter-Tribal Issues*], St. Petersburg, 1904.

97. Kh. Y. Verdiyeva, *Pereselencheskaya politika Rossiiskoi imperii v severnom Azerbaijane* [*Resettlement Policy of the Russian Empire in North Azerbaijan*], Baku, 1999.

98. *Vserossiiskoe uchreditelnoe sobraniie (1917 qod v dokumentakh i materialakh)* [*The All-Russian Constituent Assembly (1917. Documents and Records)*], Moscow-Leningrad, 1930.

99. *Zapisi grafa N. P. Ignat'eva o San-Stefano* [*Notes of Count N. P. Ignatiev on San Stefano*], S.b., 1896.

In the English Language

100. Audrey L. Altstadt, *The Azeribaijani Turks: Power and Identity under the Russian Rule*, Stanford, California, 1992.

ANAR ISGENDERLI

101. L. C. Dunsterville, *The Adventures of Dunsterforce*, London: Arnold, 1920,

102. W. E. D. Allen and P. Muratof, *Caucasian Battlefields: A History of the Wars on the Turco-Caucasian Border 1828-1921*, Cambridge 1953; the Turkish edition: Ankara, 1966.

103. Erich Feigl, *A Myth of Terror. Armenian Extremism: Its Causes and Its Historical Context*, Vienna, 1986.

104. H. Katchaznouni, *The Armenian Revolutionary Federation (Dashnagtzoutiun) Has Nothing to Do Anymore*, New York: Armenian Information Service, 1955.

105. Firuz Kazemzadeh, *The Struggle for Transcaucasia (1917-1921)*, New York, 1951.

106. Justin McCarthy, Caroline McCarthy, *Turks and Armenians: a Manual on the Armenian Question*, Washington, D.C., The Assembly of Turkish American Assosiation, 1989.

107. Justin McCarthy, "The Anatolian Armenians 1912-1922", *Proceedings of Symposium on Armenians in the Ottoman Empire and Turkiye (1912-1922)*, Bogazici University Publications, Istanbul 1984, pp 17-25.

108. Richard Pipes, *The Formation of the Soviet Union: Communism and Nationalism, 1917-1923*, Cambridge, 1964.

109. Ronald Grigor Suny, *The Baku Commune, 1917-1918: Class and Nationality in the Russian Revolution*, Princeton University Press, 1972.

110. Tadeusz Swietochowski, *Russian Azerbaijan, 1905-1920: The Shaping of National Identity in a Muslim Community*, Cambridge, 1985; Turkish translation: Ankara, 1988.

111. *Situation on arrival in Transcaucasia. Narrative of first few days in Baku. November 17th-24th, 1918* by Major General W. M. Thomson, Commanding Northern Persian Force. The British Archives, 6480105, CAB 45/107.

112. *Report of the 2nd British occupation of Baku* by General D. I. Shuttleworth. The British Archives, 6479639, WO 106/1562.

In the French Language

113. Henry Barby, *Les Extravagances Bolcheviques et L'epopee Armenienne*, Paris, 1921.

ANAR ISGENDERLI

INDEX

B

ANAR ISGENDERLI

Anar Isgenderli is a professor of history and a faculty chair at Baku State University. His research areas include history of Armenian-Turkic and Azerbaijani-Armenian relations in the Ottoman Empire and the South Caucasus in nineteenth to twentieth centuries. Among other topics, Professor Isgenderli's works investigate slaughters of Azerbaijani civilians by Armenian military detachments based on local and foreign records. *The History of Massacres in March 1918*, published in 1997, looked into reasons and outcomes of the bashing of Azerbaijani civilians by Armenian militarized gangs in Baku, Shamakhi, Quba, and other cities and towns of Azerbaijan on the basis of statistical data, interviews, and other documents completed by the Special

Investigation Commission. The 2006 treatise *The History of Turkic-Muslim Genocide in Azerbaijan (1918-1920)* analyzed available researches and records on massacres of Muslim Turks by Armenian military units and gave an objective assessment of the events. Prof. Anar Isgenderli is the author of over two hundred research articles published in and outside of Azerbaijan.

Lightning Source UK Ltd.
Milton Keynes UK

173094UK00001B/47/P